THE POWER OF THE PLACE

The Power of The Place

BY

JOAN COWEN BOWMAN

We shall not cease from exploration
And the end of all our exploring
Will be to arrive where we started
And know the place for the first time.

– T. S. ELIOT
"Little Gidding" from *Four Quartets*

THE HOMESTEAD PRESS

NEW YORK

2010

Set in Miller types
Printed by Capital Offset
Designed by Jerry Kelly

ISBN 978-0-692-00990-1

Contents

To my family, to help them understand.

ACKNOWLEDGMENTS

I came to writing late in life—in my sixties—initially at The Writing Institute at Sarah Lawrence College, where Margery Mandell first helped me hone my skills as an essayist and Suzanne Hoover identified the themes that eventually led to this book. Thanks also to Susan Thames, Carol Zoref, Charles Salzberg and Joelle Sander at the Institute who gave me ongoing constructive criticism and encouragement. In the MFA Program there, Barbara Probst Solomon, Mary Morris, Lawrence Weschler, Vivian Gornick, JoAnn Beard and Peggy Wolfson—all exceptional writers and teachers—continued to inspire me. Sarah Lawrence College turned me into a writer.

Along the way there were other positive influences. Over the years, Dr. Corinne Altenhaus, with her kindness and wisdom, helped me cut through the illusions to empower me. Olga San Giuliano (now deceased) shared with me the nuances of residential interior design. On Martha's Vineyard Island, Nancy Slonim Aronie taught me to write from my heart. Gratitude also to my son-in-law, Dr. Attilio "Buck" Favorini, Chair of the Theater Arts Department at the University of Pittsburgh, whose meticulous, sensitive critiquing of my manuscript strengthened my story immeasurably. And thanks to Diane Travers, my personal friend and classmate in the MFA Program, whose final proofreading engendered fresh revisions.

My heart goes out to Clarence and Flora Housman (the grandparents I never knew), Ruth and Eddie Cowen (my parents who had only good intentions), my brother Tommy (I wish we had been able to share our stories), and my six children, Derrik, Jim, Lisa, Teke, Bo and Jonathan (who accompanied me with patience and fortitude on much of the journey described in this book). Without all of them my story would not exist.

Certain parts of the Epilogue appeared originally in the *Vineyard Gazette* (July 31, 2009). Throughout the text I have changed a few names, but the events that unfold are etched with clarity on my chain of memories.

CHAPTER ONE

My First Skates

————

F irst rain, then icy rain, then pure ice fall through the night. The storm swirls around the mansion as I sleep ... then I wake to a miracle.

Above me, the shingle roof of the huge house creaks under its frozen coating. My bedroom windows are fringed with icicles, the panes patterned with frost. Standing on tiptoe in my flowered flannel nightie, peeking in between the crystals, I can see the front lawn stretching away—its thick green grass now a shiny, white sea, wider and longer than a playing field.

It is the winter of 1935; I am two and a half years old. I am sitting on my bedroom carpet with Rose, my Irish nanny—sitting in a sunbeam, tiny motes of dust dancing off the rug.

"Hurry, child," she urges me. "Your Da's awaitin'. He hasn't got all day, to be sure." I giggle at Rose's brogue as the two of us struggle with my quilted pink snowsuit.

Rose holds my hand as I waddle down the long, wide staircase, stiff and powerless in my puffy pink armor, my fingers immobilized by clumsy woolen mittens. The legs of my snowsuit rub together, making a funny, swishing noise with every step I take. Down the first flight I go, then across the landing, then down again. Through the banisters, I can see my father waiting for me at the bottom. He has on a bulky black parka I have never seen before; his tan leather gloves are poking out the side pockets and a little white shoebox peeks out from under his elbow. He also has on a happy face. This is very unusual; my father is a busy, serious person who most often doesn't have time for me. He and my mother live far away from me, way down the upstairs hall. He leaves for work early every morning, and usually when he comes home to have dinner with my mother in the fancy dining room, I'm upstairs with Rose—who is giving me my bath and getting me ready for bed.

Outside on the front porch, my father opens the little white box. Kneeling in front of me, he straps on a pair of silver double runners that he has rushed downtown to buy earlier that morning. I look down on his shiny, dark brown hair; I remember its oily, flowery scent intoxicating me. When he straightens up, he pulls on his gloves and lifts me onto the ice, placing me firmly in front of him. His thick leather fingertips clasp my waist and I press my mittens against them, holding my breath in wonderment, not knowing what to expect.

Before us stretches the vast, glistening sea of ice that I'd already glimpsed from my bedroom windows earlier that morning. Suddenly we are skimming across it, picking up speed as we move along faster and faster. My father's hands tighten around my waist as my double runners glide effortlessly. I feel him bending over me; I can see his breath misting with mine in the cold air; I can hear his skates just behind me, crunching in a powerful, constant rhythm. We are creating a great breeze, weaving passionately across the shimmering lawn, spiraling around the huge trees whose branches, paralyzed with ice, stretch to the ground. I can still remember feeling like a feather floating across a frozen lake, powered by a steady, secure wind. The rambling white clapboard house with its inky-green shuttered windows winks down on us like a benevolent monster.

In the center of the lawn a patch of ice has loosened in the sparkling morning sun. Over it we sail in a crescendo of speed, and I scream with delight as I hear it crackling at the edges and feel it wobbling beneath our blades. I hear my father above me, giggling at my glee. Then slowing and gliding we skate back towards the porch in front of the house. I catch my breath as we take off again—

circling around the trees, gathering momentum, soaring over the center patch in an ecstatic climax, then winding down to renew our intimate dance. My boundless bliss wipes out all sense of time; looking back, I don't know if we skated for minutes or for hours.

Back in the house we drop our icy skates and clothes in a frozen heap inside the front door. The warm air encircles my numb cheeks; my fingers and toes feel plump and pudgy from the cold. My mother is waiting for us in her corner of the big sofa, working patiently on her needlepoint. Her eyes light up when she sees my father. She beckons me to climb up onto the middle cushion. In front of us on the low table a tea tray is set for three. I have never seen this beautiful blue and white tea set before. The plates are dotted with funny-looking birds and boats and trees, and houses with pointy roofs. The teacups have lumpy gold handles; blue letters dance around the inside of each rim.

I remember crisp, crustless triangles of cinnamon toast, brown and buttery against my swollen lips, and thick, bubbly hot chocolate from the blue and white teapot. My father moves over from his red leather chair and sits close to me on the sofa. Sandwiched between the two of them, sinking back into the soft, deep pillows with my stubby legs and chubby little feet barely reaching the sofa's edge, I feel cherished and important. It seemed to me then a time of limitless love, overflowing with special promises and infinite possibilities.

I will skate many times after that, on ponds and rivers and rinks, with schoolmates, with friends, with my younger brother Tommy and even with my parents, but I will never skate that way with my father again.

CHAPTER TWO

Clarence and Flora

———

"One day in the summer of 1905," my mother loves to tell me when I'm a young girl, "my father stood across the street with me and pointed to this property—it was all woods at the time. 'Next year,' he promised, 'we'll be living over there in my dream house.'"

I imagine the two of them—my mother Ruth and her father Clarence—standing there, holding hands on a halcyon summer day. My mother's sister, Virginia, three years older, is not with them. I picture my mother in a crisply starched white pinafore trimmed in pink, with a matching pink bow adorning her blond curls. She is only three years old; her father is thirty-six.

My mother explains that the rambling, white clapboard mansion he envisioned—and where I am being brought up—was built as a summer home on its ten wooded acres, one mile in from the ocean in West End, New Jersey. My grandfather—a self-made millionaire by the turn of the nineteenth century—named his estate The Homestead, which refers to a house with adjoining buildings and land. When finished, the property boasted stables, greenhouses, a gardener's cottage, lavish flower and vegetable gardens, a charming rose garden, a lily pond and a gazebo—all carefully tended by a flock of workers, for help was inexpensive and plentiful in the early 1900s.

I love hearing these stories—though infrequent—from my mother, especially because I never knew her parents. My grandfather, Clarence J. Housman, died at age sixty-three in April 1932, a few months before I was born the following August; my grandmother, Flora Hutzler Housman, had predeceased him at age fifty-six in

1931. When my mother inherited the estate after Clarence's death, she and my father—recently married in 1931—decided to take over the mansion and the property and live there year round.

Although my parents never speak about their ancestors, and there are no signs or symbols of Judaism in the house, somehow I learn, early on, that on both sides—all the way back—my relatives are German Jews. I am never told when, why and from where in Germany they emigrated, but I know it was a long time before I was born—more than a hundred years, perhaps. Later on, I will learn that my parents are Reform Jews, and that they also have very ambivalent feelings about the faith of their forefathers.

When I'm ten or eleven I become curious about Clarence, whose austere gilt-framed portrait hangs over the dining room mantel. All I know about him is that he was born and raised in New York City, and had made his millions on Wall Street during the 1890's. One day I ask my mother if he had any siblings.

"Oh, yes," she responds, "He was one of fourteen children!"

This astounds and fascinates me, so I press her further.

"Well," she says offhandedly, "They were never all alive at the same time."

She alludes to exploding boilers and virulent childhood diseases—scarlet fever, diphtheria, whooping cough—but no additional details are ever shared. I never hear any more from her about the remaining brothers or sisters.

As a teenager, I love reading about the North Jersey Shore, and I learn that West End, a tiny village, was originally called Hollywood. It is a section of the city of Long Branch—named after the long branch of the Shrewsbury River that borders the city to the north and empties into Raritan Bay, adjoining New York Harbor. In the first half of the nineteenth century, word spread of the natural beauty of Long Branch, with its wide sandy beaches bordering the Atlantic and situated below a dramatic bluff. It gradually became a popular summer resort, noted for its boating, fishing, bathing and gambling.

As the nineteenth century progressed, hotels, private clubs, theaters, gambling casinos, upscale vendors from New York City and a racetrack—the Hollywood Track—attracted the wealthy and famous from New York, Philadelphia, and Washington, D.C., fleeing the oppressive city heat. Many chose oceanfront property in Long Branch on which to build their summer "cottages"—mansions (some boasting over twenty-five rooms) that managed to retain a homey, rustic ambiance. The city boomed; a boardwalk and the "New Scenic Railway"—an elaborate roller coaster—were added. The iron Long Branch pier could accommodate ocean-going vessels; hundreds of passengers from all walks of life traveled up and down the New Jersey coast by steamboat.

Leaders in the world of fashion, theater and politics as well as a number of our presidents and military generals also flocked to the resort in the summer months. While in office, Lincoln never traveled to the North Jersey Shore, but First Lady Mary Todd Lincoln visited Long Branch in 1861, the first year of her husband's presidency. Newspapers reported her as saying, "I have never seen a more suitable spot for a summer visit."

The list of famous late-nineteenth-century Long Branch residents and visitors is long and impressive. George Pullman, the Pullman railroad car millionaire, had a cottage on the bluffs, overlooking the ocean. His neighbors included financier Anthony Drexel, founder of what is now Drexel University in Philadelphia; George W. Childs, publisher of the Public Ledger newspaper in Philadelphia; and Moses Taylor, president of National City Bank in New York. The most famous neighbor on Ocean Avenue was President Ulysses S. Grant. In 1869, George Childs arranged the purchase of the cottage next door to his for $40,000 (almost $1,000,000 in today's market) and presented it to Grant as a gift from himself and other wealthy cottagers, who wanted him to make Long Branch his permanent summer home.

Every general in the United States Army during Grant's presidential summers in Long Branch was a guest at the Grant Cottage. Besides being a place to entertain guests informally, the oceanfront mansion was also a place of rest and retreat for the President, away from the conventions and ceremonies of his public life. Ultimately, it became the place to which he retired in 1877—allowing the sea to soothe the symptoms of his painful throat cancer. He wrote his memoirs there while rocking on the porch of the cottage. They were published shortly before his death in 1885 by his friend Samuel Clemens (otherwise known as Mark Twain), another North Jersey Shore visitor.

Grant was not the only president who sought the sea air of Long Branch for recuperation. When President James A. Garfield was shot by an assassin at the train station in Washington, D.C., in July 1881—after only four months in office—he lingered all summer until September sixth, when a special train carried him from Washington to the Elberon station. (Elberon, like West End, was another posh section of Long Branch, named after L. B. Brown, who subdivided its one hundred acres in the 1870s.) Some two thousand volunteers built a five-eighths of a mile spur from the Elberon station to the Ocean Avenue cottage belonging to Charles Franklyn, owner of the Cunard Ship Line, hoping that the stricken president would recover there from the damage inflicted by the assassin's bullet. Initially, Garfield rallied, then rapidly declined. He died in the oceanfront cottage thirteen days later on September nineteenth.

I learn from my reading that the wealthiest area of Long Branch centered around St. James Chapel on Ocean Avenue in Elberon, across from the cottage where Garfield died. In 1886, St. James claimed a congregation whose pew holders were worth a total of $120,000,000. In all, seven presidents—Grant, Hayes, Garfield, Arthur, Harrison, McKinley, and Wilson worshipped there. Known locally as "The Church of the Presidents," it still stands, now owned by the Long Branch Historical Museum.

Well-known celebrities also visited the "Branch," as Long Branch came to be known, among them actresses Maggie Mitchell, Lillie Langtry, and Lillian Russell—a famously voluptuous beauty known as the "first pin-up girl." In 1900, Nate Salsbury spent $200,000 to build nine handsome cottages on a sandy stretch of land in the north end of Long Branch for members of his world-renowned Buffalo Bill's Wild West Show. His performing troupe, which traveled across the country and also to Europe, included Buffalo Bill Cody, Annie Oakley and Chief Sitting Bull. He named the enclave The Reservation, and named each of the cottages after an Indian tribe.

Among the gamblers and bon vivants drawn to the pleasures of Long Branch was Diamond Jim Brady, who owned a cottage but also entertained lavishly, as many summer residents did, at the elegant local hotels. Brady, born in 1856, was the most flamboyant member of his generation. He was over six feet tall and enormously fat. As a sound and conservative businessman, drawing huge commissions as a salesman of railroad equipment, he had accumulated millions and soon became a Broadway showman and philanthropist. He was nationally known for his extravagant lifestyle, his huge wardrobe, his fondness for ostentatious jewelry—especially diamonds—and his enormous appetite. Whenever he appeared in public he wore formal clothes—and his collar buttons, studs, belt buckle, cuff links, scarf pin, rings, eyeglass case, lead pencil and even a removable head for his cane were all lavishly encrusted with gems. Usually he had a beautiful woman on his arm; often it was Lillian Russell, whose eating habits were reputedly a perfect match for his own. He never touched tea, coffee or alcohol, nor did he smoke. But he consumed ice cream by the quart and oranges by the dozen at a single sitting. As a before-dinner appetizer, it was nothing for him to ingest three or four dozen oysters.

The Gilded Age was the name adopted to describe the years after the Civil War leading up to the turn of the nineteenth century—the first thirty years of my grandfather Clarence's life—when many great fortunes were amassed, accompanied by opulent, excessive lifestyles. (Originally, the term was the title of a satiric novel by Mark Twain and Charles Dudley Warren, published in 1873.) Nowhere were these extravagant displays of excess more exemplified than in Newport, Rhode Island, where some of the wealthiest families in the country, such as the Vanderbilts and the Astors, constructed their palatial summer "cottages." They made it clear, however, that their society was closed; the New York City Jews of German descent, who had established enormous wealth in banking and on Wall Street, were not welcome there. Restricted from Newport, they chose Long Branch as the site of their elaborate summer homes—easily accessible by train or boat from Manhattan in the decades before paved roads and the "horseless carriage." Eventually, by the early twentieth century, the "Branch" became known as "The Jewish Newport."

The August 11, 1877 edition of the New York Daily Graphic newspaper compared the cottages of Newport and Long Branch. Although both offered a seaside location, their appearance and the lifestyle of their owners differed greatly, according to the writer. "The cottages of Newport are extensive villas and their occupants maintain them with rigor, imposing formal social customs. The cottages of Long Branch are built on a much less pretentious scale; although many are elegant they offer informality and restful independence in social observances, which the city-weary are grateful for."

Common architectural features of the Long Branch shingle-style cottages were verandas, porches, balconies, porte-cocheres, high-ceilinged rooms and large, plentiful windows—which took advantage of the cooling ocean breezes. My grandfather Clarence's mansion The Homestead incorporated all of these elements.

[9]

*

In 1869, the year my grandfather was born, the artist Winslow Homer captured the breathtaking beauty of the Long Branch beachfront in a luminous oil painting, *Long Branch, New Jersey*. In the forefront of the painting, two beautifully clothed young women with parasols stand on a bluff like sentinels, overlooking the Atlantic. Their long, layered skirts with bustles billow in the breeze, and a fluffy white terrier stands between them. Below them a row of cabanas leads to the beach, where swimmers and strollers amble on the sand. The sea is sprinkled with sailboats; fleecy pink clouds fill the endless sky. It's a breathtaking scene. I wonder if Clarence, in his youth, was familiar with or even inspired by Homer's beautiful painting.

I don't know when he first discovered "the Branch"; I like to imagine that, while growing up as a boy in New York City, he came by steamboat for the day or the weekend to visit the North Jersey Shore with his parents or schoolmates. My mother never shares the names of his parents or his father's occupation, but aside from being one of fourteen children, I also know that he and his family lived on the West Side, near where the Plaza Hotel now stands. The hotel had not yet been built, and all the acres in that area of the city were vacant lots where he and his classmates played and roved after school and where neighborhood gangs fought out their battles. The 52nd Street Gang was predominantly Irish and the toughest in the neighborhood.

Clarence attended P. S. 69 on 54th Street between Sixth and Seventh Avenues. One morning in 1880, a new boy, Bernard Baruch, from Camden, South Carolina, showed up in his sixth grade class. At noon and again at the end of the school day his teacher asked, "Will someone volunteer to take Bernard home until he knows his way to and from school?" Clarence—a chubby, serious eleven-year-old, according to Baruch—quickly raised his hand. Fourteen years later, he and Bernie would become partners on Wall Street.

Clarence's early career on Wall Street is sketchy; my mother never fills me in on any details. Without a college education he must have started out as an office boy—filling inkwells, delivering stocks and bonds, performing whatever rudimentary tasks were demanded of him—learning the securities business from the ground up. By the age of twenty-one, he was working for his much older brother Arthur Housman, who had already established a successful firm and a reputation as a shrewd wheeler and dealer in Wall Street circles.

Rummaging around in the linen closet off the second floor hallway of the mansion, I find a folder of old photographs and a handwritten note from Clarence to a friend. Dated June 3, 1890, he wrote: "Am now with [A. A. Housman] with the hope someday to be a p—. Business has been very good but the market not one to suit." Clarence must have been superstitious—not spelling out "partner" in his personal note for fear of jinxing his luck.

In his autobiography, *My Own Story*, published in 1957, Baruch wrote that in 1891, after graduating from CCNY, he was also hired by the firm of A.A. Housman, where he found Clarence, now twenty-two years old, doing all the bookkeeping. In his book, Baruch sets the scene:

> My real start in Wall Street came in 1891, when I joined the firm of A. A. Housman & Company at 52 Exchange Place. . . . Arthur A. Housman's younger brother, Clarence, turned out to have been the good-natured fat boy who had taken me to and from grammar school when we first moved to New York. Clarence kept the books of the firm. My job, which paid five dollars a week, was to act as office boy, runner, comparison clerk, and general utility man.
>
> I opened the office in the morning and saw that the inkwells, pens, and the blotter on Mr. Housman's desk were in order. Then I took the books out of the safe and put them on Clarence's desk. I copied the letters, indexing them in the

copybook, and helped get out the monthly statements. I also had to be on hand, when the runners came in, to check on anything that remained to be done.

In those days there was no stock clearing house. Each and every share sold had to be delivered by 2:15 P.M. the following day. On the northwest corner of Exchange Place and Broad Street stood a building, several stories high, filled with brokers' offices. Up and down those stairs we boys would clatter, making our deliveries. I would shove a bundle of securities through the cashier's window, crying out, "Hold the check for Housman," and rush off to make the next delivery.

By 1895, both Clarence and Bernie had become partners in the firm. Eventually, World War I took Baruch out of Wall Street and into public affairs. After serving as chairman of the War Industries Board, he was called to Paris by Woodrow Wilson to help draft the peace treaty. He went on to become the "park bench advisor" to every U.S. President until the end of World War II—his photograph frequently popping up over those years in newspapers and magazines. He married an Episcopalian, raised two daughters in New York society, and also had a well-publicized affair with Pamela Churchill Harriman when she was a young thing on her way up the social ladder. In 1946, he was the architect of an unsuccessful plan put forward by the United States for the international control of atomic energy, offering what he called "a choice between the quick and the dead."

I don't know exactly when their lifestyles diverged, but Bernie's ambitions were much more grandiose than Clarence's, who had no interest in national politics or international fame. He was a successful Wall Street investor, and when he aspired to the life of a country gentleman, he hired Harry Allen Jacobs, a prominent Manhattan architect, to design his manor house on the North Jersey Shore. I assume he was thoroughly content with his wife and two daughters, his Wall Street partnership, his newfound wealth and his country estate.

An undated article from a New York City newspaper that I found in an old family scrapbook celebrates his success. The headline reads: "EXPERT IN MONEY MARKET. Clarence J. Housman Regarded as Astute Judge of Conditions—Axioms for Brokerage Houses." Surrounding a pen-and-ink sketch of my grandfather in front of a ticker tape, the text reads:

> Clarence J. Housman is now the senior partner of the Brokerage firm of A. A. Housman and Co., of No. 20 Broad street. Aside from being a great "business getter" Mr. Housman is regarded as one of the Wall street experts in judging money market conditions. He has laid down a principle which all his associates and partners accept as axiomatic to the effect that the customers make a brokerage house and that the brokerage firm should not dictate or attempt to guide customers in their operations.
>
> Mr. Housman is fond of horseback riding and other athletic diversions. His great pride is in his summer home at Elberon, N. J., where he raises poultry with more or less success. Some of his friends assert that he is the handsomest man in the loan crowd on the Stock Exchange.

My mother has a briefer explanation for how her father had made his money in the late 1800s. "There was no federal income tax and there was no SEC. Wall Street speculators—shrewd ones like my father—made and kept their millions," she tells me.

Clarence did involve himself briefly in local politics, serving as mayor of Long Branch for one term after his retirement from Wall Street in the early 1920s. On May 18, 1920, the Long Branch Daily Record reported that the newly elected city commissioners had named Clarence J. Housman as mayor. The Record noted: "Before entering the council chamber, the . . . commissioners held a short conference in the mayor's office. They were greeted with cheers as they assembled in public meeting. . . . A bunch of roses and a fountain pen were handed the mayor. They were the gift of the West End Engine Company."

On February 4, 1924, during his last year in office, the Record featured a proclamation by Mayor Housman commemorating the death of former president Woodrow Wilson. In part it read: "Mr. Wilson, while president, was for a time one of our fellow-citizens, and from here his second victorious campaign for the presidency was conducted. Hence, Long Branch and New Jersey as a whole especially mourn the passing of this great soul."

My grandfather then went on to request that all flags be flown at half-mast in the city and that businesses stay closed until after Wilson's funeral. Wilson had visited "the Branch" frequently during his two terms, residing at Shadow Lawn, a palatial stone mansion not far from The Homestead that became known as the Summer White House. It was across the street from Solomon Guggenheim's one-hundred-room Italianate Aladdin's Palace; certain super-millionaires on the North Jersey Shore were reverting to the Newport style of summer cottage.

A photograph shows Clarence standing in front of City Hall with two fellow politicos. "He said it was the worst job he ever held," my mother tells me. During his four-year tenure, he was shocked by the bribery and corruption—even on a small-town level—and vowed never to become involved again in anything as distasteful as politics.

I'm also curious about my grandmother, Flora, five years younger than Clarence.

"She was a Hutzler from Baltimore," my mother tells me proudly.

The Hutzlers are an old, well-established family of Jewish merchants who own Baltimore's leading department store. My mother never explains how the two of them met and courted, but she does comment on the marriage.

"In those days it was almost scandalous for a young woman from Baltimore to marry someone from as far away as New York."

Later, as a teenager, when I recall this remark, I wonder if my mother—and her father before her—are embarrassed about his humble beginnings in a sprawling, uneducated family on the west side of Manhattan, and don't wish to acknowledge them. Since my grandfather, Clarence, married "up," I conjecture that the "scandal" really involved an impeccably pedigreed Baltimore Hutzler marrying a young, nouveau riche New York City upstart.

My mother's most dramatic reminiscence about her parents revolves around their trip in September 1901 to the Pan-American Exposition in Buffalo. President McKinley (another Long Branch summer visitor) had been re-elected in 1900 by a large majority to a second term, having defeated Spanish forces in Cuba and on the seas in the brief Spanish-American War of 1898. He was ending his post-election tour of the country at the Exposition. On September 6 at four o'clock in the afternoon, my grandparents were standing in line at a public reception at the Temple of Music, waiting to shake hands with him, when a shot rang out. The man in front of them, a twenty-eight-year-old anarchist from Detroit, had attempted to assassinate the President, hiding a pistol in his heavily bandaged hand. He was later linked to well-known anarchist Emma Goldman, an outspoken American radical who had emigrated from Russia in 1885. One of her chief doctrines was that all leaders should be eliminated.

According to a newspaper article at the time, two shots were fired at the assassin "before the miserable wretch was brought to the floor ... where he lay ... his face bleeding ... his breath coming short ... His eyes rolled now and then to the ceiling and his limbs twitched nervously."

The newspaper report continues:

> Here in this vast sorrow stricken assemblage ... was truly exemplified the bond of sympathy which links all mankind. No man was weak who wept; it was the time for weeping. Women were no more affected than men. They clung close to each other; it was a moment when everyone felt he needed help. Help of any kind, only a word, a look, that was all.

McKinley was taken in an electric ambulance to the Emergency Hospital on the Exposition grounds. Five of the most distinguished physicians in America were sent to his bedside, but on September 14 he died at the age of fifty-eight. Flora must have been in her fifth month of pregnancy when she witnessed the assassination, since my mother was born on January 29, 1902.

From my mother I also gather that Clarence and Flora liked to hobnob with the rich and famous. Her favorite anecdote recalls Diamond Jim Brady's visit to The Homestead as a dinner guest during her childhood. Since Brady was renowned for his gargantuan appetite, my grandmother's larders were overflowing and the kitchen staff was fully prepared for the occasion.

"Much to everyone's surprise," my mother loves to relate, "Diamond Jim ate sparingly—even less than the other guests."

My grandparents learned several days later that whenever Brady was invited to dine in a private setting, he always downed an enormous meal beforehand—to avoid embarrassing his host and hostess.

Other stories leak out. Flora had a brother, George Hutzler, an independently wealthy bachelor who lived in a brownstone at 21 West 52nd Street in Manhattan. After World War I he decided to put his townhouse on the market and move to Paris. Some years later, during the height of Prohibition, he returned to New York City for a visit. Friends picked him up at his hotel and headed for "the hottest new speakeasy in town." A few minutes later, much to his astonishment, their taxi pulled up in front of "21," his former home on 52nd Street.

Weird, fascinating relatives float in and out of my childhood days at The Homestead. My father's oldest brother, Uncle Harry, is married to a Parisian, Aunt Agnes, who claims that her belly-button is off-center—the cause of many chronic ailments. When they visit, my father, who has no patience with her, declares—behind her back—that she is "absolutely nuts." His older brother, Uncle Arthur, is married to Aunt Rosalind, a glamorous figure whose bedroom in their townhouse on East 74ᵗʰ Street is sheathed in silver wallpaper. They also have a summer house on Ocean Avenue in Elberon, and when Tommy and I are very young and our parents are away on vacation, Aunt Rosalind invites us for lunch where we are introduced to exotic foods—artichokes, avocados, squab, duckling—that we have never tasted before and aren't sure how to handle.

Later on, I learn that Uncle Arthur has a roving eye and engages in extramarital liaisons. This explains why occasionally, after a flurry of phone calls, my father, looking grim, leaves our house for Arthur and Rosalind's house in Elberon—to soothe Rosalind's ruffled feathers and attempt to keep their marriage together.

My father's oldest sister, Aunt Mabel—almost blinded by childhood scarlet fever—lives in an apartment in the Stanhope Hotel across from the Metropolitan Museum of Art in Manhattan and is married to an elderly, wobbly Southern gentleman—Uncle Gene, from Culpeper, Virginia. They come to The Place once or twice a year for a weekend. My parents have told Tommy and me that Uncle Gene wears a toupee, and we always agree to try to knock it off—or at least askew—by greeting him with exuberant hugs. Gene always wards us off with his elegant silver-tipped cane.

My father's older sister, Aunt Violet, has also married a Southerner and lives with him and their two children in Atlanta; Aunt Violet and Uncle Huntz also visit us in New Jersey once or twice a year. They are warm and friendly and I wish I could spend more time with them. When I'm thirteen, we drive south to visit them during summer vacation; I'm reading *Gone With The Wind* in the back seat of the car, following the course of the Civil War as we wend our way through Virginia and the Carolinas towards Atlanta. My father is very put off by Violet's thick Southern accent. "What a phony! She's a New Yorker, born and bred, for God's sakes!" he exclaims to my mother when out of Violet's earshot.

I remember my mother telling Tommy and me one summer's day that Aunt Antoinette Hutzler was coming for lunch—someone we had never met before. Her most distinctive feature is her dyed navy-blue hair—as shiny as patent leather—which my mother describes to us before her arrival, hoping that we won't stare. Antoinette arrives wearing a broad-brimmed straw hat, which she never removes. While she and my mother have drinks on the porch before lunch, Tommy and I plunk ourselves down at her feet like puppies, craning our necks—to no avail—for a glimpse of a few navy-blue strands under the hat. My mother is supremely embarrassed by our behavior; my father, when he gets home from the office and hears about it, finds it hilarious.

Most of these houseguests bring us presents, and soon after they arrive, Tommy and I trail them upstairs to their guest rooms, hanging around in the hallway, listening for the metallic snap of suitcases opening (luggage always snapped open in those days before zippers were applied to suitcases), then patiently awaiting the presentation of the gifts. Since friends and relatives of my parents know I'm a reader, books are commonplace. A more memorable gift during those childhood years—from an old bachelor friend of my father's—is a Kodak Brownie camera. Another favorite is the Jumbo Box of Crayola crayons—fifty colors, including gold, silver and copper, packed tightly in the trademark yellow-and-green box. Many of them have exotic names that I add to my vocabulary—magenta, cantaloupe, hyacinth. That box of crayons sets me off on a lifelong love of color.

*

Once or twice every summer, my mother announces to Tommy and me, "We're calling on Uncle Fred this afternoon."

Uncle Fred and his wife, Aunt Stella, live in New York City in winter but spend the summer months in a large vine-covered mansion near the ocean in Elberon. Soaped and scrubbed after a morning at the beach, Tommy and I sit silently on their front porch sipping lemonade under an awning of wisteria while my mother chats nervously away. I have the distinct feeling that she does not look forward to these social calls but she never explains. My father does not accompany us on these visits. Over the years I learn that Uncle Fred's last name is Housman; that he is one of Clarence's brothers; that he is very rich from his career on Wall Street but that Aunt Stella is richer; and that the only reason we visit is to ensure that the three of us will be mentioned in their wills.

Uncle Fred raises orchids in his hothouse in Elberon, but he is better known for his close resemblance to Monty Woolley, a famous Hollywood character actor with an imposing demeanor and wonderful white whiskers. People are always coming up to him, in restaurants, in shops, even on the streets of Manhattan, asking for his autograph. Uncle Fred always complies, signing "Best regards, Monty Woolley," with a flourish.

He also has a habit of snitching small items from the shelves of the local Gristede's near his apartment in Manhattan and the neighborhood market in Elberon, stuffing them surreptitiously in his pockets. Aunt Stella has an understanding with all the store help, who secretly keep their eyes on him and then bill her privately for the "stolen goods."

"Uncle Fred doesn't know that everyone is onto his little game," my mother comments on our way home, a contemptuous tone in her voice.

*

My mother doesn't like the stern, stiff portrait of her father Clarence in the dining room; I'm guessing it doesn't reveal his true spirit. I imagine him as fun-loving and flamboyant and a bit of a bon vivant, and I know we would have had a good time together.

[19]

She never shares her feelings about Clarence and Flora with me, nor does she ever comment on their marriage or how they raised her. But I savor her nuggets of family history, storing them away in my impressionable young memory like shiny new pennies in a piggy bank. However, I'm not satisfied with the meager information about Flora that I had collected from her in my curious phase when I was ten or twelve. One day, a few years later, when I'm home from boarding school and alone with my mother's oldest friend, Lize, who lives on Pullman Avenue in Elberon, I ask for her recollections.

"She was so stylish and elegant. And she had very extravagant taste in clothes." She looks at me and smiles. "And the most beautiful gray-green eyes. You've inherited her eyes, Joan."

I ponder all of this. Flora and I are exactly alike, I decide, and I know she would have understood me more than anyone else in the whole wide world.

Growing up on The Place, I wonder how different life would be if Flora and Clarence were there—taking part in my childhood. I imagine that Flora would have told my mother to get rid of Mamzelle, my Swiss governess, with her strict, unloving ways. She would have taken me shopping for a special outfit—perhaps a winter coat with a fur collar and muff. Clarence would have taught me to ride, and would have bought me my very own pony. They would have taken me to the movies with them, and out for an ice cream soda afterwards on the way home. We would have traveled to Manhattan together, where Clarence would have shown me his office on Wall Street; we would have gone to a Broadway show and stayed overnight at an elegant hotel uptown. I know they would have listened to me—to my hopes, my dreams, my feelings. They would have given me everything that I needed.

A photograph on a table in the living room shows the two of them standing in front of their beloved house. It must be only a few years after it was built; they appear to be in their late thirties or early forties. They look very dapper—he in knickers and high stockings, she in a long, pleated, plaid skirt and belted cardigan sweater, shielding her eyes from the sun. In another picture they are strolling confidently on the boardwalk, he in a full-length raccoon coat, she in beaver with a matching fur hat.

I stare closely at their faces in these photographs, trying to capture some essence of their personalities. But the camera, as inscrutable as my mother, reveals nothing of their inner selves.

Sometimes life can be lonely for me on The Place, with missing, make-believe grandparents—and real parents who live far away down the upstairs hall, and don't always seem to care.

My grandfather's dream house, 5 years after it was built, summer 1911.

My grandparents, Clarence and
Flora Housman, in front of the
house, circa 1911.

Portrait of Clarence, age 19, dated 1888.

Dear Leon,

We remove this day from our old home to 68 West 75 St. Would have let you hear from me before this but have been so busy could not find the time. Am now with the above firm, with the hope someday to be a p—. Business has been very good tho, the market not one to suit.

Hope to see you soon in our new home! Will you be up this summer? Have not seen your friend M. S. Hoping to hear from you soon,

Your friend
Clarence

Letter from Clarence, age 21, to a friend, hoping for a p— (partnership), dated June 3, 1890.

EXPERT IN MONEY MARKET.

Clarence J. Housman Regarded as Astute Judge of Conditions—Axioms for Brokerage Houses.

Clarence J. Housman is now the senior partner of the brokerage firm of A. A. Housman & Co., of No. 20 Broad street. Aside from being a great "business get-

CLARENCE J. HOUSMAN

ter" Mr. Housman is regarded as one of the Wall street experts in judging money market conditions. He has laid down a principle which all his associates and partners accept as axiomatic to the effect that the customers make a brokerage house and that the brokerage firm should not dictate or attempt to guide customers in their operations.

Mr. Housman is fond of horseback riding and other athletic diversions. His great pride is in his summer home, at Elberon, N. J., where he raises poultry with more or less success. Some of his friends assert that he is the handsomest man in the loan crowd on the Stock Exchange.

Article celebrating Clarence, now a partner at A. A. Housman and Company, date unknown.

Portrait of Clarence, date unknown.

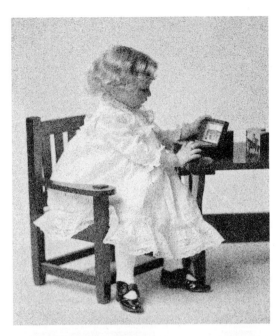

My mother Ruth Babette Housman (born January 29, 1902), circa 1905.

Ruth and her older sister Virginia, circa 1908.

Ruth, Flora and Virginia in front of the house, circa 1910.

Graduation from The Finch School (Ruth standing second from left), early 1920s.

My father Eddie (Edwin A. Cowen, born March 8, 1893), the youngest of 5.
Clockwise: Harry, Arthur, Mabel, Violet, Eddie, circa 1895.

Ruth with Virginia at the wheel in front of the house, circa 1918.

Eddie, age 15, (back row first on left), Columbia Grammar School, NYC, 1908.

Eddie, a lieutenant in the Artillery Corps, with an Army buddy, circa 1918.

Eddie in his Army uniform, probably at Plattsburgh, circa 1916.

Clarence, mayor of Long Branch, flanked by 2 politicos, circa 1924.

Clarence and Flora with a friend on the Long Branch boardwalk, late 1920s.

CHAPTER THREE
My Kingdom

For some unknown reason, as far back as I can remember, I always referred to The Homestead—in my mind—as The Place. And during my childhood, before the outbreak of World War II, The Place—both the mansion and the property—was my magical kingdom. Life there, during my first ten years, was far removed from the real world outside its winding gravel driveway and stone gateposts.

The house was filled with big, high-ceilinged rooms; wide windows looked out on the expansive acreage and its large, leafy trees—pine, oak, maple and purple beech. The spacious living room, its walls paneled in ash, was furnished with comfortable, overstuffed furniture, some of it left over from my grandparents' time. The room had an informal, undecorated look, with velvety, pale green wall-to-wall carpeting, faded chintz at the windows, and muted homespun plaids and tweeds on the sofas and chairs. Family photographs and albums were scattered on tables around the room; in front of the big sofa an old sleigh bench served as a coffee table.

The living room was flanked at one end by a very formal dining room, where my grandfather's portrait above the mantel was complemented by hand-painted Chinese wallpaper, a shiny black vinyl floor, a pewter chandelier and mahogany Hepplewhite furniture. Under the dining table was a little brown box with a button that allowed my mother, at the touch of a toe, to summon Margaret, our downstairs maid, from the adjoining pantry when she and my father were ready for the next course from the kitchen, where Gerda, our cook, presided. The crystal water goblets were cobalt blue, and at dinner, between the main course and dessert, matching blue finger bowls were served. I longed for the day when I could dip my fingers like a grownup into my very own finger bowl, but my brother Tommy—two years younger—and I were not invited to dine with my parents at the mahogany table under the pewter chandelier until we were teenagers.

Instead, at mealtimes, we were relegated to the "card room," a small, casual room at the other end of the living room where my mother held weekly games of mahjong and canasta in the afternoons, where both my parents listened to the news on the radio in the evenings, and where they often played bridge with friends. Margaret would bring our food from the kitchen to the card room on a large tray, and our Swiss governess Mamzelle (short for Mademoiselle) would eat with Tommy and me at the bridge table. She was Rose's replacement, brought into the household when my mother decided the two of us were too old for a nanny.

From the living room, the pale green carpeting wound its way up the wide staircase to a broad landing, then up another flight of stairs to the long, open second-floor hallway. Here, six airy bedrooms were filled with old furniture, flowered wallpapers and fluffy white organdy curtains tied back with porcelain knobs. Two of them—the master bedroom and the largest guest room—had adjoining porches; each one had its own bathroom—a veritable luxury when the house was built in 1906—and a paneled door of ash closing it off from the hall, as well as a louvered "summer door," that ostensibly allowed the cooler air rising up the stairway to circulate into the bedrooms on hot summer nights.

Tommy and I were in two separate rooms at one end of the hallway, supervised by Mamzelle, who babbled orders at us in French. *"Dépêche-toi, Tommy! Tu sera en retard comme toujours!"* ("Hurry up, Tommy! You'll be late as usual!") *"Vite! Vite! Le petit déjeuner est prêt, Joan."* ("Hurry up! Breakfast is ready, Joan").

Nearby, a sitting room had been converted into a playroom, filled with all our toys and games and our small brown radio, which we especially loved. On Saturday mornings we listened to *Let's Pretend*; on Sunday evenings Jack Benny, Fred Allen and Edgar Bergen, a ventriloquist who conversed with Charlie McCarthy—a very funny puppet—were favorite comedians with their own individual programs. Mamzelle had a big, comfortable club chair by the window, where she knitted, sewed and read after our bedtimes.

My parents were all the way down at the opposite end of the hallway, in a corner bedroom whose windows—when wide open—caught the sea breezes in the dog days of summer, with a bathroom and my father's dressing room adjoining. This was the bedroom that my mother had shared with her sister Virginia when they grew up in the house. She chose to share it also with my father, turning the original master bedroom at the top of the stairs—much closer to Tommy and me—into the "big guest room." This and the "little guest room" were frequently occupied by friends or relatives of my parents who loved to visit The Place. In each one, the night table was equipped with a little brown buzzer that rang in the servants' wing if breakfast or extra towels or an afternoon drink were desired.

My parents also had a buzzer, which summoned Margaret to bring their breakfast upstairs on a tray each morning. On weekdays, my father—dressed for work in a custom-tailored three-piece business suit—would sit in a chair sipping his freshly squeezed orange juice and coffee, constantly fingering the gold pocket watch in his vest, checking the time so as not to be late for his commute to Manhattan by train. My mother would still be in her nightgown, a bed jacket thrown around her shoulders for warmth.

Inside the house, there was always something to explore. In a corner of the living room, behind the coat closet, my grandfather—after a series of strokes in his old age—had installed an Otis elevator. It was off limits to Tommy and me, but we sneaked rides with Margaret and her trays, pushing the black up and down buttons, hoping to get stuck halfway so we could try the fearful, never-used red emergency button. This never happened, but it kept us in a brief state of suspense on our journeys up and down. On the third floor, a musty attic was filled with warped, creaky furniture, old leather suitcases, and steamer trunks—cracked and weathered from my grandparents' many transatlantic crossings. In the cellar a huge iron furnace growled and hissed like a prehistoric monster; spooky, dark closets housed discarded Christmas decorations, rusty old sleds and skates and dusty bottles of wine.

Outside the house, a long veranda, with a terra cotta tile floor laid evenly in large squares and a tongue-and-groove ceiling painted sky blue, stretched across the facade of the mansion. The front porch, as we called it, was sprinkled with sisal rugs and dark green wicker furniture left over from my grandparents' day—the same color as the shutters of the house. The wicker had been repainted many times, and I loved to sit and finger the little bumps of paint that had collected over the years in between the woven slats. In the summer months matching inky-green flower boxes overflowing with bright red geraniums dotted all the porches, upstairs and down, and morning glories in azure blue and deep purple climbed the portico near the front door, opening and closing their faces to the summer sunlight.

At the far end of the front porch a green wicker swing was suspended from the ceiling. This was a favorite spot for me in the summer months—for swinging back and forth with a good friend or a special book, the salt drying in crumbly patches on our freckled, suntanned skin from our morning swims in the ocean and saltwater pool at the Ocean Beach Club in nearby Elberon. I loved all the A. A. Milne books about Winnie the Pooh, and Lewis Carroll's *Alice in Wonderland*, and Francis Hodgson Burnett's *The Secret Garden* and *The Little Princess*, and especially Robert Louis Stevenson's *A Child's Garden of Verses*. His poems and illustrations were quaint and old-fashioned, but my thoughts and feelings were reflected in all of them. I would read the verses over and over again until my favorites were as familiar to me as an old tune.

Often, in the early summer evenings, my parents and their friends would gather around the wicker swing for cocktails, followed by dinner on the adjoining screened-in eating porch that looked out over the gardens. Their gentle buzzings and occasional cacklings would drift up through my bedroom windows, lulling me to sleep and reminding me of my most favorite Stevenson poem, "Bed in Summer":

> In winter I get up at night
> And dress by yellow candlelight.
> In summer, quite the other way,
> I have to go to bed by day.
>
> I have to go to bed and see
> The birds still hopping on the tree,
> Or hear the grownup people's feet
> Still going past me in the street.
>
> And does it not seem hard to you,
> When all the sky is clear and blue,
> And I should like so much to play,
> To have to go to bed by day?

Across the property there were many seasonal surprises. Bursts of color from forsythia, azalea, lilac, dogwood and magnolia signaled the arrival of spring. Peach and cherry and apple trees were there for the picking through the summer and fall months. In June, a circular bed of lily of the valley bloomed around the dappled trunk of a huge oak tree; I would lie on my back among the delicate white flowers and let the fragile fragrance drift over me. Over the summer months in the garden beds, strawberries nestled under hay, ripe for nibbling; baby carrots could be wrenched from the soil, rinsed under a nearby garden hose and munched on; fresh peas could be plucked from the vine and eaten, pod and all. Close by, in the center of a secluded rose garden, a tiny lily pond was framed by a weeping willow tree, its tender branches trailing in the water. Pear trees were espaliered against an old brick wall nearby. A greenhouse was filled with moist and mysterious pots and plantings, and tucked away on a bulletin board, a collection of faded and frayed blue and red ribbons boasted of garden prizes from a bygone day.

In the fall, after school, we would throw on our play clothes and recklessly jump in and out of the huge leaf piles raked up by the gardeners. As the days grew shorter, the giant holly bushes near the front door, bulging with plump bunches of scarlet berries, forecast the delights of the Christmas season. After the holidays, we would wait expectantly for the winter storms—waking in the night to hear the snowflakes whispering against the windowpanes, praying for the early morning phone call announcing the cancellation of school, then rejoicing in the day of fun ahead. Bundled against the cold we would spend hours transforming great drifts into igloos and creating clans of snowmen on the front lawn.

No matter what time of year, there was always magic for me on The Place. I was familiar with every inch of the house and the ten-acre property, but my idyllic days there were marred by the presence of Mamzelle and my mother's approval of her. Mamzelle shared my bedroom and also my bathroom, where her peculiar underwear, ribbed and spoked, slept on a small bench next to the tub. She chauffeured Tommy and me to school, to music and dancing lessons, to doctors and dentists, and introduced us to the intricacies of French verbs and pronouns and vocabulary. I resented her existence and longed for a "real" mother, not a short, stocky substitute whose broken English and blithering French embarrassed me. When we were out and about I liked to pretend she was a distant relative from the old country; I always tried to walk a few steps in front of her, which gave me a certain inner satisfaction. And I discovered another subtle way to retaliate. My mother wanted me to converse with her in French and become comfortable with the language, and although I gradually came to understand every word she spoke, I insisted in answering her in English. *"En français, en français, je t'en prie!"* she would exclaim. ("In French, in French, please!") But I persisted in my private little rebellion.

Once, at supper in the card room, when I was eight or nine years old, in an attempt to break me of the habit of sniffing Gerda's delicious food before tasting it, Mamzelle pushed my face into a bowl of beautiful, steamy green pea soup. Angry and humiliated, I sat swallowing my rage, watching my large salty tears fall into that suddenly unappetizing puddle of chartreuse. As far as I knew, no one ever told my mother about this incident, and I certainly didn't have her ear. I knew that if I tried to share it with her she would rebuff me and take Mamzelle's side. I had sensed early on that she didn't want to hear about problems, especially complaints from either of her two children. Nothing was allowed to interfere with her "perfect" life on The Place with my father.

I had no idea how Mamzelle felt about me; like my mother, she never shared any intimacies. I found her stern and strict, not affectionate and loving. I hated her for invading my privacy; I hated my mother for hiring her and being so selfishly dependent on her; I hated both of them for never considering my feelings. But I was afraid to rebel; I knew I had to endure their cruelties. Looking back, I must have been terrified that if I retaliated I would lose whatever tiny teaspoon of attention and affection I desperately hoped we shared.

But they couldn't take my magical kingdom away from me—with all its sounds and colors and smells and tastes. My very own special world. All mine.

CHAPTER FOUR

Ruth and Eddie

———

"I'm so lucky ... I have the happiest of marriages ... I'm truly blessed." My mother tells me this over and over again during my childhood, but it has a hollow ring to my ears. I know we live in the most magical surroundings, but if hers is the happiest of marriages, why am I not the happiest of children?

My mother, Ruth Babette (she hated her middle name, but I thought it was old-fashioned and cute) was born in 1902 in New York City. She and her sister Virginia, three years older, spent their winters in Manhattan and summered in West End. They did not attend school but were tutored at home in the manner of the English upper class. Virginia was beautiful, flamboyant, and spoiled. "Virginia was a party girl," my mother told me any number of times, with a disdainful sniff. A party girl, I later figured out, also meant an incipient alcoholic.

They were tall and slim, blonde and big-breasted, the two Housman sisters, but unlike Virginia, my mother Ruth was not beautiful. Also, unlike her older sister, who was spoiled and temperamental, my mother was sweet and shy and stable. She told me that she had stuttered severely as a child, and that Clarence and Flora had doted on Virginia. I think of her as the "ugly duckling" of the pair.

Virginia married in 1919 when she was twenty years old. She and her husband moved into The Little House—a smaller home on The Place that my grandfather had built for them as a wedding gift. The Little House was only "little" in comparison to the mansion; in many ways it was a miniature version of the big house, with a lovely front porch, a living and dining room, three upstairs bedrooms clustered together, and a small servants' wing over the kitchen.

Virginia's husband, Freddie Spiegelberg, had served during World War I as a lieutenant in the American Air Service in France; when he married her the year after the Armistice, he returned to the family fur business in New York City. My mother described him as extremely good-looking and charming; she also told me that the marriage was laced with violent arguments, triggered by Virginia's self-centered ways and probably incited by excessive drinking. Freddie was also an amateur poet; I found a book of his war poems, *Crimson Days*—self-published in 1919, the year of his marriage—in my mother's bookcase. On the title page was a handwritten inscription in black ink: "To Ruth—with the kindest regards of the author." Below this another inscription was scrawled in green ink: "Three months later: The dearest little sister-in-law—prospective. 'Tried and found true.'"

My mother was seventeen at the time of Virginia's wedding, living with her parents year-round and eventually attending Miss Finch's, an exclusive two-year finishing school housed in adjoining brownstones on East 78th Street. The school catered to the daughters of wealthy families who had limited intellectual aspirations and were not yet engaged or married. In a graduation photograph, she is standing in the back row flanked by seven other classmates—all wearing simple white frocks and white shoes, holding huge sprays of flowers, looking like a bevy of bridesmaids. My mother is tall and slim with huge eyes and a narrow aquiline nose, her hair carefully coiffed in the style of the early 1920s—a handsome young woman, but not a beauty.

My mother's oldest friend Lize—like my mother, unmarried at the time—vividly remembers driving home to Elberon in the fall of 1924 with her father after a Princeton football game. This was a popular diversion for residents of the North Jersey Shore, even though the university was more than fifty miles away over bumpy, unpaved roads. About halfway home, they came to a dead stop behind a long line of cars. Lize's father decided to walk ahead to see what the trouble was, and some time later he reappeared with Ruth and Virginia in tow. They, too, had been returning home from the game—my mother to the mansion where she was living with her parents, Virginia to The Little House with Freddie—riding in the back seat of an open touring car with Freddie in the front passenger seat and a friend of his at the wheel. They had run off the road, and Freddie, thrown from the car, was killed instantly. The driver, drunk, was uninjured.

Virginia was hysterical and was eventually taken to a local hospital where she suffered a miscarriage. She and Freddie already had a three-year-old girl, Ginny, born in 1921, who fortunately had not accompanied them that day. But Lize was particularly struck by my mother's reaction. "She was absolutely frozen," she told me many times when recounting the story to me. "She had just been through a terrifying accident, her brother-in-law was lying dead in a ditch, her sister was out of control. But she just sat there with us in our car, showing no emotions at all."

My mother was twenty-two years old when Freddie was killed and Virginia widowed. She was twenty-eight, still living with my grandparents, Clarence and Flora, when she met my father, Edwin Cowen, and he began courting her. They were married in March 1931, shortly after my grandmother Flora's death—in a small ceremony held at the apartment at the Warwick Hotel in Manhattan that Clarence and Flora owned—and drove to The Cloisters in Sea Island, Georgia, to spend their honeymoon. The country was in the grip of the Great Depression; driving home they heard on the car radio that the Federal Reserve Board had ordered all the banks to close down. "It was a frightening time," my father recounted to me years later. "I wasn't sure I had enough cash in my wallet to make it back to New Jersey."

When my grandfather died in 1932, my mother inherited The Place; my parents decided to take over the management of the estate and live in the mansion permanently. Virginia was still widowed, living in The Little House with her daughter Ginny. She was drowning her sorrows in alcohol; eventually her condition deteriorated to the point where she was drinking all the perfume and Listerine from her medicine cabinet. When she left for treatment, Ginny came to live temporarily with my parents, her Auntie Ruth and Uncle Eddie. In one of my mother's scrapbooks, a snapshot shows me—eight weeks old—propped up in my mother's lap on a rocking chair in her bedroom, with Ginny—eleven years old—next to us, looking over at me adoringly. Two years later in 1934, Virginia, now in recovery, married Aaron Berg, a graduate of Columbia and a New York City lawyer. In 1935, another girl, Carol Jane, was born into the family next door in The Little House.

I have a very clear recollection of Virginia and Aaron's wedding, which took place in the living room in the mansion when I was two years old. I distinctly remember my frothy white dress (it must have been organza) and white Mary Jane shoes. The living room was filled with white flowers, and the alcove where the spinet piano usually resided was framed with an arbor of the same flowers. When I was ten years old, I proudly shared this memory with my mother.

"Joan!" she exclaimed. "You were barely two years old! You couldn't possibly have remembered *anything*! You've just heard other people talking about it!"

I already knew that I couldn't complain to my mother; now I knew that she had rigid opinions, and more importantly, had no respect for mine. I told myself I would have to be careful with whatever I shared with her. I felt betrayed and humiliated, but it never occurred to me to fight back. I would adopt this passive mode of response and reluctance to defend my views for many years.

A few years later—after the war ended—when Tommy and I

were allowed to have dinner with my parents in the dining room and were privy to their discussions, we soon learned that my father had no respect for "Uncle Aaron." Most of his dislike was centered on Aaron's tardy payment of the bills they shared in the management of the estate—property taxes, landscaping charges, gardeners' salaries. One evening at the table my brother, who had a quick wit, whimsically nicknamed him the A-Bomb; he was the A-Bomb *en famille* until the day he died many years later, in 1978.

*

Everyone always knew that The Place meant everything—absolutely everything—to my mother. It also became very clear to me, early on, that she would go to the ends of the earth for my father. She never mentioned any other suitors to me—I think he was the only one. She was completely willing to give herself up to this handsome, genteel man nine years her senior, making no demands on herself. He was her knight in shining armor; I believe he saved her from spinsterhood.

Later, when I was older, I often wondered what she would have done if she had had to choose between my father and The Place, but fortunately that circumstance never arose. There were, however, confusing messages.

"You know, your father never wanted children ... .I talked him into having a family."

I was seven or eight years old when my mother first divulged this to me, but if I heard it once I heard it a thousand times. She said it with a quiet pride, a smug sense of accomplishment, and I hated her for not realizing that it invalidated my existence. She also had a habit of announcing it to various friends and acquaintances in front of my brother Tommy and me. "Eddie never wanted children," she would declare, looking over at the two of us as if we were a pair of little miracles. Her declaration echoed in my mind—never wanted children, never-wanted-children, neverwantedchildren—a jumble of words, both meaningless and self-defining, that over the years became my mantra.

My father, born in New York City in 1893, the youngest of five—the baby of the family—had been doted on by his mother, whom he adored. "She spoiled him to death," my mother remarked countless times, and continued to do the same thing, perpetuating the attention his mother had fostered on him. It was easy to understand why he didn't want children accessorizing his marriage; he wanted to be the centerpiece.

He was almost forty years old when I was born—an elegant post-Victorian gentleman, possessed with enormous warmth and charm, which he saved, for the most part, for the outside world. At home, he was often distant and depressed. My brother, skinny and sickly as a young child, mumbled and stammered and never seemed able to please him. I was plump and reliable; I wanted to please everybody and always tried to do everything right. I frequently had my nose in a book.

Once in a while, a truly dark spell would come over my father. For several days, he would not speak to anyone in the house. My mother always put on a cheery face, chattering about inconsequential things, pretending that all was right with her world when I knew that everything must be falling apart. It certainly was for me—I felt like running away and hiding until the torture was over. I hated her for patronizing him and putting up with these black moods, which terrified me. I wanted her to confront him and tell him that he was making life miserable for everyone around him. But she completely ignored his melancholia, waiting it out. How could my mother claim to have "the happiest of marriages" when my father behaved this way?

Despite his distant ways, my father told me a lot about himself. He had attended Columbia Grammar School, a private boys' school in New York City, where he had played on the ice hockey team. His education there was steeped in Latin and Greek, and he loved to recite the opening verses of Homer's *Odyssey* to me, extolling the musicality of the ancient Greek language. As a teenager, he had traveled a great deal with his older brother, Arthur, and had taken the entrance exams for Princeton University in 1908 while vacationing in Berlin at the age of fifteen. In those days a high school diploma was not a prerequisite for entrance into college. His two older brothers had graduated from Columbia, his oldest sister from Barnard. "My father was running out of money and wanted to get my college expenses over with," he explained to me, a tone of disrespect in his voice.

This was one of the few times he ever mentioned his father George Cowen to me; I believe he was in the glass business. I suspected that he was a poor businessman and possibly a philanderer; my father was not forthcoming. But he loved to talk about his mother. "Everybody loved Ma Cowen," he would tell me. "And everybody called her Ma." She had a habit of taking stray people—charity cases—into her house in West End, giving them shelter until they got back on their feet. "I never knew who might be sleeping in the attic—or sometimes even for a few days in my own room," he related with a chuckle. I could hear the love and admiration in his voice. I dimly remember visiting Ma, when I was very little, in her summer house not far from The Place—a sweet old woman wearing thick glasses, her white hair pulled back in a bun. She died soon after.

My father was accepted at Princeton, the youngest member of his class, surrounded by freshmen two or three years older than he. As a Jew, he was restricted from joining an eating club, the cornerstone of undergraduate social life at that time. His roommate, a close childhood friend who was also Jewish, was called home sophomore year to run the family business after the sudden death of his father. My father recalled his years at Princeton as painful and isolating, but something about the college got under his skin. Perhaps it was the cloistered beauty of the campus, or the brilliant and inspirational professors, or a desperate desire to truly belong to this prestigious, hallowed place on every level possible. In later years, as social boundaries dissolved, he established close relationships with many classmates and became an ardent alumnus, devoutly attending football games and class reunions. He was finally accepted and respected, no longer an outsider; this was supremely important to him.

In 1913, one year before the outbreak of World War I and the year the federal government imposed the first income tax, he graduated from Princeton. When the United States entered the war, he applied to Officers' Training School in Plattsburgh, New York, near the Canadian border, graduating and serving in France at the front during the final three weeks before the Armistice as a second lieutenant in the artillery.

*

Day-to-day life on The Place was stable and predictable. My father was totally absorbed with the activities of the small Wall Street firm, Cowen and Company, which he had founded with his two older brothers in the early 1920s. He was very thankful and proud that the fledgling firm had survived the Crash of 1929 and the ensuing Great Depression, when so many other companies had foundered. He had a keen mathematical mind and was very intellectually involved in his work, bringing a scientific approach to financial investments; he was an "analyst" before Wall Street had coined the phrase. My mother was totally dedicated to sustaining a hedonistic world for the two of them to bask in—surrounded by servants, overflowing with comforts, as free from problems as possible.

On weekdays and sometimes on Saturdays (the Stock Exchange was open on Saturday mornings before World War II) my father would leave the house punctually to catch an early morning train to the city. During the week, by the time he arrived home shortly after six, Tommy and I would have finished our supper with Mamzelle in the card room. Then we would be allowed to visit my parents in their bedroom, where they rested up before going downstairs for dinner in the formal dining room. They would be stretched out on the twin four-poster beds that were pushed tightly together, and we would spread ourselves across the crack, trying to get close to them.

Lying across the beds, I would play with my mother's glossy, scarlet, beautifully manicured fingernails. If she was going out to dinner she would let me pack her handbag for the evening—transferring her lipstick, comb and compact from her daytime handbag, filling her elegant gold and lapis lazuli cigarette case with Lucky Strikes, and choosing—with infinite care—a hand-embroidered handkerchief from the freshly ironed pile in the top drawer of her dressing table, making sure its colors matched her outfit. I loved her clothes, faintly tinged with Arpege, and I nicknamed them by their buttons—the butterscotch blouse, the peppermint dress, the snowflake suit.

Occasionally my father would complain of a headache from his daily trials at the office. I would kneel next to him on the bed and massage his forehead. This was the closest I ever got to him. He also had a playful side, seldom revealed to us. But one evening on the beds, he was relating the events of his day to my mother when he mentioned a Mr. Bernstein. For some reason, my brother and I found this surname hysterically funny and were both doubled over with laughter. Even my parents got the giggles from our giggling. For some time afterwards—maybe a year at most, before he tired of it—my father invented an imaginary character by the same name who lived on the ceiling. I distinctly remember the three of us hauling Bernstein down onto the beds with an imaginary rope and extracting several of his teeth.

I was aware that my father had very strong opinions, which he occasionally shared but never took the time to explain to me. I knew that he hated Franklin D. Roosevelt, and he also made fun of Eleanor, whom he considered a very homely woman. When I took up the habit of biting my fingernails, he would chide, "Take your fingers out of your mouth, Joan. If you keep that up you're going to grow up as ugly as Eleanor Roosevelt!"

He had a good ear for music and often brought songbooks and sheet music home from the city. As I approached adolescence, we would play together—I on the piano and he on his mandolin—all the popular songs of his day and my day, from Romberg, Kern and Rodgers and Hart on up through Gershwin, Berlin, Porter and Rodgers and Hammerstein. "Stardust," "Embraceable You," "Summertime" from *Porgy and Bess* and "As Time Goes By" from the film *Casablanca* were among his favorites. Privately, with a teacher and lessons once a week, I was struggling with Bach and Mozart and Chopin, but he showed no interest in my progress, nor did my mother. They never asked me to perform for them. Instead, my father and I would play his favorite songs over and over again. As popular Broadway shows and Hollywood musicals continued to open—*Oklahoma*, *Carousel*, *Brigadoon*, *Finian's Rainbow* and *State Fair*, among others—more and more sheet music would come home in his brief case. My father seemed very content sitting in a chair next to me at the piano, depending on me to explain what key we were in and how many sharps and flats he would have to tackle.

Around this time—when I was eleven or twelve—my father shared a "secret" that I revealed to no one for many years. We were strolling in the neighborhood on one of our Sunday morning walks. Suddenly he started talking wistfully about an aristocratic young Cuban woman he had met in Havana when traveling there with his older brother Arthur in the 1920s.

He described her to me as beautiful and charming, then explained that because of religious and cultural differences he could not seriously court her. It was clear to me—even though I was young and naive—that he was still in love with her, or at least with the memory of her. I was shocked. But I said nothing; I just listened.

"We were never alone together," he went on. "She had to be accompanied by a duenna—it was the custom."

Then he added in a comforting tone, "But your mother and I have built such a wonderful life together ... ." His voice trailed off as we ambled along.

His "secret" filled me with tempting fantasies that made me resent my own mother even more. I imagined myself with an exquisite, exotic Cuban mother, being fully fluent in Spanish as well as English, and partaking of the fascinating rituals of the Catholic Church, which Rose, my Irish nanny, had already exposed me to when—as a very young child—I accompanied her to Sunday Mass. I also found his confession hauntingly disturbing. I wasn't convinced about his "wonderful life" with my mother. Although the two of them seemed quietly compatible, I wasn't aware of anything truly passionate between them. I knew my mother "adored" my father, but his confidence revealed—for me—an emotional compromise on his part, and I felt uncomfortable being privy to it. His "secret" confirmed that he had missed out on something big, something really important. Why would he confess this to me, his only daughter, and how much had he told my mother?

If she knew, perhaps she felt triumphant, for after all, she had won her man. Or maybe her knowing explained why she would never confront my father's inner demons when his moody, dark side took over. Maybe she sensed a tenuousness in their relationship and feared that if confronted he would become enraged and leave her.

During her lifetime, my mother never once spoke to me about my father's earlier loves. But a few years after she died, a cousin of mine—Ginny's daughter Nancy—told me that on her side of the family it was common knowledge that Eddie had married my mother on the rebound. "Oh yes, I know," I responded. "The Cuban lady." Nancy shook her head. "It was someone in New York City, but I don't know her name."

*

When I was fourteen years old and entering ninth grade, I left The Place for boarding school in Bryn Mawr, a suburb of Philadelphia. I understood that the local high school would not prepare me properly for the high-powered college education my parents envisioned for me; with their approval I had chosen The Baldwin School, a well-established, well-respected girls' school, founded in 1888, over several others we had visited the previous year.

My parents drove me to Bryn Mawr on opening day; I was very nervous and excited, but not at all sad about leaving home for the first time. While saying goodbye to them in the Main Hall of The Residence—an imposing, turreted edifice that had originally been built in the 1800s as the fashionable Bryn Mawr Hotel—my mother started to cry. It was the first time of only two times in my entire life that I ever saw her shed a tear. A few days later I received a letter from her, apologizing for her "selfishness." Apparently the only loving feelings that she was willing to acknowledge were towards my father. I always wondered if she truly loved me.

Nevertheless, she wrote faithfully to me every week, chatty, friendly letters, and occasionally my father would write. I had the feeling that my mother talked him into corresponding. He always signed his letters to me "Your Loving Father." Those were the only words of affection I ever heard from him, and they always brought tears to my eyes.

Years later, I learned that my father had confided to a close friend his fear that I would grow up to become a "bluestocking"—an old-fashioned term for a woman, usually a spinster, with scholarly or literary interests. That was before I went away to school, when I was plump, shy and self-conscious, and frequently had my nose in a book. As a teenager, when I grew tall and slim and strikingly pretty, I guess other fears took over. Whether bookworm or beauty, he just didn't seem to know what to do with me.

Something profound always haunted him, but I never found out what it was. Perhaps he was obsessed by a longing for his unrequited Cuban love, or for the woman in New York City who had spurned him. Perhaps some unspeakable brutality witnessed during the war had fractured his spirit. Perhaps his depressiveness was caused by his ongoing social circumstances as a Jew—by the anti-Semitism he must have endured not only at Princeton but also later during his Wall Street career, although he never shared the latter with me.

I have never been able to figure out what inspired him to sweep me away on that glittering lawn of ice that magical winter's day when I was three. I cannot remember him ever holding me again, cannot recall ever again feeling his passion and his power, cannot remember another time with my mother and father filled with that perfect sense of belonging.

CHAPTER FIVE
In the Back of the House

———

Behind the swinging dining room door the servants' wing opened up, room after room, as large as the front of the house but different in every aspect. In between the pantry and the kitchen with its adjacent laundry room and maids' dining room, a dark, steep stairway led to six small bedrooms and one bathroom on the second floor. A second bathroom was tucked in an alcove halfway up the steep staircase. This wing of the house was most recognizable to me by its smells, more serious and utilitarian and pungent than the delicate floral scents in our part of the house. Furniture polish, laundry soap and cleaning fluids mingled with the redolent odors of roasts and pies, all drifting up the back stairs from the kitchen below.

When I was very young, some of my best friends lived in this warren of tiny rooms on the second floor above the kitchen. Elizabeth, the upstairs maid, had immigrated from Norway as a young girl; she was old and wrinkled and left over from my grandmother's day. When I was older I heard that she had once given birth to a stillborn child. I remember her as small and sweet; she gave us funny nicknames.

"Good morning, Joanie-baloney," she would greet me at breakfast.

"Hi there, Tommy-salami," she would say, giggling at my brother.

Margaret, the downstairs maid, who waited on table in the dining room, was a big, strapping, cheerful young woman, American-born of Hungarian descent. Gerda, the good-natured cook, spoke with a heavy Swedish accent and shared several rooms at the end of the wing near the bathroom with her husband, John, a carpenter, who drove to work off the property each day, leaving behind a trail of sweet-smelling smoke from his ever-present pipe.

[53]

Looking back, I suspect that this little colony of servants, living in such close quarters, must have encountered many internecine squabbles and misunderstandings, but I don't remember ever hearing any dissension. I yearned to be part of their world, which seemed warmer and friendlier than the world in the front of the house, and I entered into it every chance I could get.

In mid-February every year my parents would leave for their annual six-week vacation. Usually they drove to Phoenix, Arizona— "motoring" my father called it—and stayed at the Arizona Biltmore, a famous resort designed by Frank Lloyd Wright. Although they drove a Packard sedan, not a covered wagon, they seemed to approach their trip with the zeal of the pioneers in their prairie schooners. For several weeks before their departure, they would spend hours poring over road maps and consulting their bible, The Duncan Hines Guide. Years before he was a mainstay on the bakery shelves of supermarkets, Hines was crisscrossing the highways and byways of every state in the U.S.A., testing out inns and hotels and restaurants and reviewing them in his books for adventurous motorists.

As they ventured west, a sporadic series of picture postcards arrived, apprising Tommy and me of my parents' whereabouts—initially mailed from little-heard-of towns sprinkled across the heartland. My favorite ones followed after they arrived in Arizona—puffy mailings that cascaded when opened with color photographs on both sides. These I perused, many times over, trying to grasp a piece of their life together away from us. I carefully studied seasonal views of the Grand Canyon, close-ups of the Indian tribes of the Southwest in native dress and an assortment of blooming cacti indigenous to the North American desert.

My parents never told us much about their travels, but I distinctly remember them giggling once on their return about dilapidated hotels and sheets infested with bedbugs. Their most astounding discovery one particular year was the existence of a hotel where you could park your car right outside your room. It was called a motor lodge or "motel," they told us—a name they found immeasurably clever.

They were always absent for my father's birthday on March 8th, and for their anniversary on March 18th. Prodded by Mamzelle, Tommy and I dutifully prepared our homemade cards for mailing. On a background of carefully chosen colored paper, we would glue a timely Kodak moment—the two of us in front of a recently constructed snowman, or skating merrily on a nearby pond. Our final flourishes were crooked messages, hand-printed in our finest grammar school penmanship, using our favorite Crayola colors. Back then, Hallmark was not a household word.

While my parents were away, draperies and curtains would be removed for cleaning and laundering; sofas and chairs would sometimes disappear for reupholstering. Mr. Claude, the housepainter, would arrive and shroud all the remaining furniture in the front of the house with sheets. He would move his ladder from room to room, painting and papering, chattering away and cracking jokes with my brother and me as he prepared the house for my parents' return in early April.

During those weeks we took all our meals at the kitchen table; there was always something simmering on the stove, and Gerda would be up to her elbows in flour, baking goodies for my brother and me. My favorite concoction was her mocha cake, the inside white and feathery from seemingly hours of hand beating, the filling and frosting pale brown, grainy and glistening—a secret combination of chocolate, coffee, sugar and butter.

The production of the cake would start in the morning hours, heralded as we left for school by Gerda presiding over of a parade of crockery mixing bowls on the kitchen table, interspersed with her weapons of choice—glinting stainless steel eggbeaters and clunky wooden spoons.

"Ve vill finish ze cake ven you get back," she would whisper with a smile, as I straggled out the kitchen door with my book bag and lunch box.

By the time we returned mid-afternoon, the cake—already baked and cooled and covered with icing—would be waiting for me to apply the finishing touches. Gerda would instruct me to dab little dents all over the cake's top and sides with the back of a spoon, creating an overlapping scallop pattern. When my decorating efforts were complete, I would lick the spoon with my tongue and swipe my fingers around the icing bowl, smacking them clean. The cake would then sit splendidly on the table until demolition at dinnertime.

I loved it in the back of the house, and didn't really care if my parents ever came back. I could even tolerate Mamzelle during those weeks my parents were on vacation. She couldn't babble in French because Gerda, Elizabeth and Margaret wouldn't have been able to converse with her. Instead, she softened and seemed to enjoy their company. With my mother and father away, her strict, stern demeanor relaxed; she stopped making demands on Tommy and me and ordering us around. During those six weeks in the kitchen, I felt wrapped up in sweetness and warmth and light, and I savored every minute of it. Life was cozier, and even the food tasted better, in the back of the house.

*

Out the kitchen door and across the property in a far corner, Jerry, the gardener, lived in a tiny cottage with his wife and two young sons, Arnold and Gary. On summer days he would bring fresh flowers into the pantry for Margaret to arrange in the front rooms, and fruits and vegetables into the kitchen for Gerda to incorporate into our menus. Above the stables, which had been converted into a two-car garage complete with gas pump, Carter, the chauffeur, lived with his wife and two young sons, Buddy and Bobby. Carter had a first name—Harold—but everyone on The Place and in town called him Carter. He was a master mechanic, in charge of maintenance on our cars. He was also responsible for driving my father to the station for his morning commute, and during the school year, for taking Tommy and me to a tiny red brick schoolhouse eight miles away from The Place.

Carter had another very important duty to perform, be it only once a year. Like many Reform Jews of German ancestry, my parents had assimilated all the secular trimmings of Christmas. The holiday was a major event in the household; our tree in the living room reached all the way up to the twenty-foot ceiling. On Christmas morning Carter secretly dressed up as Santa Claus and handed out gifts to all the children who lived on The Place and came with their families to gape at the huge tree. One year, my brother and I peeked through the pantry keyhole when my parents weren't watching and saw him plumping up his wiry body with pillows, his Santa suit and beard crumpled up on the counter behind him. My mother heard us giggling in delight over our discovery and swore us to secrecy "for the sake of the other children."

Christmas was magical in many ways, but it was lonely, too. On Christmas Eve, Tommy and I would hang up our stockings above the fireplace in the living room and then be packed off to bed early. My mother embraced the Santa Claus myth with the zeal of a young child, and she wanted us to believe that he landed on the roof, came down the chimney, filled our stockings and trimmed the tree—leaving our gifts under it to be opened Christmas morning. This was fine when I was very young; I would fall asleep listening for the jingle bells announcing Santa's landing on the rooftop. But by the time I was seven or eight and realized the truth about Santa, I wanted to be downstairs with my parents and their close friends (including my father's Princeton roommate who lived around the corner with his brother), helping to decorate the huge tree, watching the grownups open their gifts, and maybe even opening one or two gifts of my own. Lying in bed, listening to the rustling of Christmas wrappings and the happy chatter of the grownups, made me feel left out and unimportant.

And sometimes the presents from my mother and father were disappointing, after all the waiting and anticipation. One year, when I had outgrown my two-wheeler and needed a bigger size, I asked for a sleek racing bike with thin tires and a gearshift on the handlebars. Instead I found—parked under the tree on Christmas morning—the same bike (with fat tires and no gears) that I had already had, one size larger. My biggest disappointment came the year I asked for white figure skates instead of the ugly, low-topped black skates with racing blades—just like my brother's—that I had always worn. I knew exactly what these skates looked like, having watched my idol Sonja Heine—a beautiful, blonde Norwegian figure skater who had won three Olympic medals and become a movie star—in all her Hollywood films. What showed up under the tree was a cheap imitation of the "real" skates that I had been hoping for. I felt as if my parents never really listened to me—or if they did, they didn't really care about my dreams and desires, and just did what was easiest for them. Maybe they'd even sent Carter or Mamzelle to pick out these major gifts.

During Christmas vacation they would always drive Tommy and me, one evening after our supper with Mamzelle, to Interlaken—a nearby town that was famous for its Christmas lights. Sitting in the back seat of my father's black Plymouth sedan—his station car—I would press my face against the window as we wandered up and down the winding streets. There were no large properties here, and I would stare into the front windows of house after house, desperately wishing that I lived in one of these snug little homes, trying to catch a glimpse of a "real" mother and father and family. I expected them to be seated together at the dining room table, and I could hear their conversation in my head. The mother would be wearing an apron; the father, home from work and still in his shirt and tie, would compliment her on her cooking. Flanked at the table by his young son and daughter, he would question them about their school day and their homework assignments, and tell them about their next vacation together. They would all be smiling. I knew what these people looked like; I had seen them on Norman Rockwell's covers of the Saturday Evening Post in my parents' bedroom.

Back in the mansion, while my mother and father settled down for cocktails in the living room, followed by dinner in the formal dining room, Tommy and I would get ready for bed upstairs under Mamzelle's watchful eyes. *"N'oubliez-pas tes prières,"* ("Don't forget your prayers,") she would remind me as she tucked me in for the night.

Closing my eyes, I would dutifully whisper to myself, *"Notre père qui est aux cieux ... "* ("Our father who art in heaven ... "). The words would trail off as I drifted to sleep, imagining cheerful, homey Christmases surrounded by "real" mothers and fathers in my favorite bungalows.

CHAPTER SIX

Wars

———

I'm six years old, strolling with my father on the Long Branch boardwalk. It's a bleak, blustery Sunday in January. The beach is barren below us; whitecaps dance on the choppy, gray sea. The bitter smell of approaching snow hangs in the air. My father is telling me his war stories.

"It was 1918—only twenty years ago," he reminds me. I'm in first grade, and he knows I haven't learned to subtract yet. He's talking about the last three weeks at the French front during World War I; he was a lieutenant in the artillery near Verdun. He describes spending the night with his exhausted men in a dark, abandoned barn, then waking up in the cold, early daylight to discover that he has fallen asleep on the corpse of a German soldier. The terror in his voice gives me goose pimples.

"I promised myself that if I ever got home to a warm house and clean sheets I would never complain again—about anything," he tells me.

"Eleven, eleven, eleven," he chants, as we walk along. "That's when the guns were silenced—on the eleventh hour of the eleventh day of the eleventh month. Armistice Day." I know about Armistice Day— we have a holiday from school.

My father catches his breath, then lets out a deep sigh. "Sixty-thousand of our men dead ... the Great War ... the War to End all Wars."

*

I'm nine years old, playing hide-and-seek in the back yard of my best friend's house with my younger brother and her older sister. It's late on a Sunday afternoon, warm for early December. "Ollie-ollie-in-come-free!" we shout at each other, the four of us darting between the hedges and trees in the deepening autumn shadows. We're having fun, and we don't want to go in when the grownups summon us.

Inside the house, we gather together to hear President Roosevelt's voice crackling over the radio, pronouncing this Sunday—December 7, 1941—"a day of infamy," then officially declaring war on the Empire of Japan. Around me the adult voices are murmuring, ". . . nothing the same . . . ever the same . . . nothing will ever be the same."

Overnight, it seems, everything changes. Ugly cement Coast Guard towers are erected on the cliffs above the beaches; we hang black-out curtains on all the windows and dim down the lights after dark. There are rumors of German submarines off shore and possible air raids. Sugar, butter, meat, leather and gasoline are rationed; my mother learns to ride a bicycle and rides off to a volunteer job at the local Rationing Board. By the time spring and summer of 1942 arrive, she and my father are pedaling their bikes on weekends to their golf club— five miles each way—to keep up their game. In the evenings they ride off to nearby dinner parties—no longer "black tie," since tuxedos and long evening dresses are not compatible with travel on a two-wheeler.

With car travel limited because of the gasoline shortage, Tommy and I savor a new sense of freedom. We love to bike around town doing errands for my mother. That first summer of the war we also love riding the five miles round-trip to and from our beach club in Elberon—where we frolic in the ocean for hours and take our diving and swimming lessons in the saltwater pool, just as we did before the outbreak of the war. But back at home, a map of the world on the wall of the playroom is a constant reminder of the fighting in both the Atlantic and the Pacific. We listen to the news on our radio and move little tacks around on the map, denoting where all the ongoing battles are taking place. Strange, hard-to-pronounce place names are continually entering our everyday vocabulary, starting off with El Alamein, Bataan and Corregidor.

Everything changes on The Place, too. Margaret joins the WACS and meets her future husband in the Army, coming back after the war to raise a family in a nearby town. Carter and Jerry go off to work in defense plants, resettling their families and never returning to the property. On Christmas Day 1942, my father takes Carter's place and dresses up as Santa Claus, but the enchantment is over. None of us believes in Santa any more. The world is at war, and nothing on The Place will ever be the same.

As the months wear on and we continue to ride our bikes around town—to the post office, the hardware store and the beach—little navy-blue-and-white banners with one red star, and sometimes more than one, start showing up in the front windows of shops and houses, showing that a family member has joined up and gone off to war. It isn't long before a red star is replaced by a gold one, showing that a member of the family has been killed in action. Once in a while two gold stars appear on a single banner.

Somehow, when I think back on those three-and-a-half war years, only those banners are in Technicolor; everything else appears in newsreel black-and-white. The grownups talked incessantly around us about the war, day-in and day-out. It was a dark and sad time, seemingly with no end in sight. To paraphrase a popular song we heard often on the radio, we were all waiting for the lights to go on again, all over the world.

*

One morning in February 1945, six months before the war ended, we went downstairs, collected our book bags and lunchboxes, and waited for Mamzelle to drive us to school. My mother was standing by the front door talking quietly to two policemen. "Your father's been in an accident," she said nonchalantly. "Don't worry. I'll see you this afternoon when you get home."

At school I became absorbed in all the activities I loved and forgot about the two policemen at the front door. When the school day ended, Tommy and I ran out of the building and jumped in the car for the ride back to The Place. Mamzelle took one look at us and burst into tears. Usually she was bossy and stern; I couldn't imagine why she was crying. She kept muttering in French, over and over again, *"Quel catastrophe! Un homme extraordinaire! Si gentil! Si généreux! Si brave!"* ("What a catastrophe! Such an extraordinary man! So lovely! So generous! So fine!") Until that moment, I had never had any idea that Mamzelle harbored such warm, caring feelings for my father.

We drove directly to Monmouth Memorial Hospital in Long Branch—the hospital my grandfather had helped found, where Tommy and I had been born—only two miles from The Place. In between her tears and outbursts, she answered our questions about the early morning accident.

Apparently my father had been running late for his regular train. Frank the gardener—an Italian immigrant who had permanently replaced both Jerry and Carter and who lived over the garage with his young wife, Jenny—was chauffeuring him in the black Plymouth sedan. It was a bitterly cold day, and when they reached the tracks at the West End station, they discovered that the gates were frozen open. The gateman was nowhere in sight, but they stopped, looked, and listened, and waited for the southbound train from New York City to pass by. Then they immediately started crossing the tracks and were instantly hit by the train my father had hoped to catch, which had just pulled out of the station heading north for the city. The locomotive plowed into the passenger door on my father's side of the Plymouth; he took a direct blow from the steam engine. The car, totally demolished, was saved from turning upside down when it smashed into the gateman's hut on the driver's side. It all happened in a split second.

At the hospital we took the elevator to the sixth floor. The tiny waiting room was filled with the faces of my relatives and my parents' friends. Some of them had been on the train that had crushed my father and his car that morning. They rushed over to me, shaking my hand, kissing me and cooing their condolences. I had known these people all my life, and couldn't imagine why they were suddenly being so sweet and kind.

Someone took me by the hand and led me into my father's room. He lay on his back in the hospital bed, completely helpless; his right leg was immobilized in some sort of metallic contraption; his head, slightly elevated, was wrapped in bandages. A deep cut over his right brow had been tightly stitched and his right eye was half-shut and crinkled. He looked like the scarecrow in *The Wizard of Oz*— my favorite movie to date. But I had never seen him like this before. My father had turned ugly and scary.

As I stood by the side of the bed, he mumbled something to me and reached out his hand—as if to soak some strength and energy from me. I was shocked—ordinarily he never touched me. I tried to say, "Hi, Daddy," but my eyes were swollen with tears and the words clotted in my throat. My heart was bursting with terror. I suddenly knew why all those people were out there in the waiting room. My father was going to die, and they had come to keep vigil with my mother.

Frank suffered a concussion and permanent damage to his eyesight; he lived with double vision for the rest of his life. My father's injuries were more complex—a fractured femur, shattered where it connected to his pelvis; facial lacerations; a serious concussion; and severe traumatic shock, which kept him at death's door for forty-eight hours. But he pulled through those delicate first two days, and embarked on a long and agonizing convalescence.

Over the ensuing weeks, my mother and my father's brother, Arthur, conferred at length with various hospital doctors. Hips were being pinned experimentally in New York City and Boston, with no assurance of success. With only local roads available (the Garden State Parkway and the New Jersey Turnpike had not yet been constructed), it was decided that a transport to either city would be extremely distressful and possibly dangerous to my father's condition. A conventional approach to his hip injury was chosen.

He spent three months on his back with his leg in traction at Monmouth Memorial—and his lengthy hospitalization became a routine part of our daily lives. My mother dedicated herself to his recovery, dutifully spending her days in his corner room on the top floor, with its soothing, expansive views of the ocean. Tommy and I would visit every afternoon after school, bringing him the latest news from the European and Pacific fronts. I would stare out the windows at the sea stretching endlessly to the horizon, thinking of all the people dying three thousand miles away.

In March, after bitter fighting, our flag was raised on the island of Iwo Jima. My father's fifty-second birthday passed on March 8. When the bandages were removed from his head, his thick, straight, dark brown hair was shot with gray.

Through March and April the Allied troops advanced eastward in Europe and began the occupation of the German homeland. My father developed painful bedsores from lying immobilized for so many weeks. But his relentless rehabilitation continued. By early April he was being wheeled on a stretcher to physical therapy every morning, returning to bed exhausted after an excruciating session of manipulation.

On April 12, on our way to the hospital after school, we heard on the car radio that President Roosevelt had just died in Warm Springs. Driving down Broadway, the main street of Long Branch, we saw people sharing the unexpected news with each other. Many were weeping. At the hospital, we rushed into my father's room where he was napping, brimming over with our latest bulletin.

He was no fan of Roosevelt's to be sure, but the news greatly disturbed him. "How on earth is that funny little haberdasher from Independence, Missouri, going to run this country—and the war?" He shook his head in disbelief. It was beyond his imagination that Harry Truman could possibly go down in history as one of our more outstanding presidents.

Hitler committed suicide on April 30 as Soviet troops encircled Berlin; on May 8 the German surrender was signed. Coincidentally, it was Truman's sixty-first birthday; it went down in history as V-E Day. By now my father was taking his lunch sitting up in a chair near his bed.

He had been home for only a few weeks and was learning to walk again with a cumbersome brace and crutches when Okinawa was captured in June. Jimmy Doolittle led strategic bombing raids over Japan in July, and rumors of a possible invasion of the Japanese inlands were rampant.

By early August, when the deadly bombs were dropped over Hiroshima and Nagasaki, my father was limping into the saltwater pool at our beach club every morning—his physical therapist from the hospital at his side. Painfully stretching and bending and kicking, supported by the buoyancy of the water, he kept trying to get his damaged leg working again.

My father's battles were not over when V-J Day ended World War II on August 15 that summer. He remained crippled for the rest of his life, in constant pain unless he was sitting or lying down. The injured leg was permanently shorter than the other; he would never be able to skate, or ride a bike, or even walk at a fast clip again. Stairs were impossible for him, and my grandfather's trusty Otis elevator in the corner of the living room behind the coat closet was pressed into daily service.

Despite his painful handicap, I never heard my father complain or even discuss his misfortune. Perhaps he was consciously living up to the promise he had made at daybreak on that brutal morning near Verdun in November 1918—the promise he had shared with me when I was six years old: "If I ever got home to a warm house and clean sheets I would never complain again—about anything." And I never heard my mother complain, either. Perhaps in the privacy of their bedroom they shared their thoughts and came to some mutual understanding about what came to be known in the family as The Accident. My mother often referenced it obliquely in conversation: "That was the Christmas before The Accident" or "that was the summer two years after The Accident." It certainly had to have been a major turning point in the calendar of her life, but her devotion to my father never faltered. And she never said anything personal to me about that fateful February day that turned her husband into a cripple—anything emotional or philosophical or self-pitying—anything at all.

Over the twelve months following V-J Day, before I left The Place for boarding school in early September 1946, my father slowly turned back into the handsome, elegant, distant man I remembered from my younger years—albeit with a serious limp. He gradually resumed commuting to work at Cowen and Company, and returned to the golf, travel and social activities he had always indulged in with my mother. Looking back, I think The Accident may have brought them even closer together, as he became more and more dependent on her due to the restrictions imposed by his handicap.

Eventually a thickly built-up, clumsy orthopedic shoe compensated for the shortness of his damaged leg. For the rest of his life my mother would have to tie my father's shoelaces for him. Somehow, for me, this image of her bending over him is emblematic of their relationship—she as his handmaiden, always at his beck and call, always there to help. Such a good sport, such a trouper.

Joan Mary Cowen (born August 19, 1932). I'm 6 weeks old in my mother's arms on The Place, September 1932.

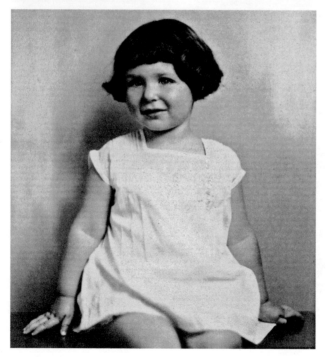

I'm 3 months old,
November 1932.

I'm 2 years old,
1934.

Tommy (Edwin A. Cowen, Jr., born October 12, 1934), my mother and me, 1936.

At my father's 25ᵗʰ Princeton Reunion, June 1938.

On my sixth
birthday, August
19, 1938.

I loved this navy
blue velveteen
dress with
grosgrain belt,
circa 1938.

Tommy and me, Halloween, 1939.

(above) Ready for the horse show, age 8, summer 1940.

(right) A blue ribbon at the horse show. (The stables closed after the onset of World War II in 1941, ending my short-lived riding career.)

Graduation Day at The Baldwin School, Bryn Mawr, PA, June 1950.

(above) My mother, Mamzelle and me at lunch after graduation.

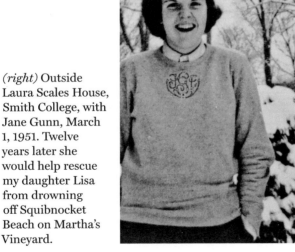

(right) Outside Laura Scales House, Smith College, with Jane Gunn, March 1, 1951. Twelve years later she would help rescue my daughter Lisa from drowning off Squibnocket Beach on Martha's Vineyard.

Tommy on The Place,
summer 1951.

My mother, Tommy and
me in front of the house,
summer 1951.

Graduation Day with Rowdy Crew members Mildred "Mud" Mooney (center) and Barb Wilson, Smith College, June 7, 1954.

Red (soon to be my husband) with me on The Place, summer 1954.

Summer and winter views of The Place, taken in 1947 from The Little House next door by Ginny's husband Bill Kahn.

CHAPTER SEVEN
The Jewish Dilemma

———

"**J**udaism has its roots in justice and revenge," my father is telling me in a critical tone. "An eye for an eye, a tooth for a tooth." "Christianity is based on mercy and forgiveness." He states this with approval in his voice.

The two of us are sitting at the end of the front porch waiting for lunch, and he is lecturing me. It's late August 1946; in a few weeks I'll be leaving The Place for The Baldwin School, a girls' boarding school on the Main Line near Philadelphia. I've just celebrated my fourteenth birthday, and will be starting ninth grade.

I've heard his theory about the major difference between the Jewish and Christian faiths before. But sitting with me on the porch today, knowing that I will be going away in September to a boarding school whose day-to-day values are based on Christian principles, my father has a more practical reason for addressing his religious views with me. He knows that I will be expected to attend church services with my classmates every Sunday. (If I were an observant Jew I would be excused from this and would be allowed to attend synagogue every Friday evening.) When he settles back in his green wicker chair and stretches out his bad leg, I know he has more to say.

"You're going to have a unique opportunity at Baldwin, Joan—a chance to investigate other religions. I want you to take advantage of that over the next four years."

In June I had finished eight years at the Shrewsbury Grammar School, a small, red brick schoolhouse eight miles from The Place. My parents had discovered the school when they learned that the Long Branch public schools had a lackluster reputation and would not prepare me properly for boarding school. The classes at the

Shrewsbury School were small, and the teachers gave each student a lot of personal attention. Tommy and I were among the few who were driven there from outlying communities; all the other students who lived in the two-square-mile town of Shrewsbury walked to and from the building. Not one of them had a governess.

This made me feel even more like an outsider than living behind the stone gateposts on The Place. But from my very first day in kindergarten, I loved the smell of school—a pungent combination of chalk, erasers, paint, glue, pencil shavings, ink (real ink, since the ballpoint pen had yet to be invented), floor polish, disinfectant, new books and old books. A few months after I started, my parents were summoned by my teacher Miss Hamm (I loved her name, since ham was Tommy's favorite food) and told that I was to be promoted into her first grade, which shared a room with the kindergarten. For a number of weeks, I had been ignoring the work on my maple slant-top desk, avidly engrossed in the first-grade work that was ongoing in the aisle across from mine.

I loved all the maps and learning about the world; I loved reading the stories and the poetry. Science was boring; arithmetic became increasingly difficult and dreary. Music and art were the most fun and my favorites. But most of all, after my lonely existence on The Place, I was fascinated by my classmates: beautiful Carly Niles, whose father was a newspaper reporter and whose mother (according to my father) was even more beautiful than Carly; brainy Patsy Kinloch who loved to sketch and wanted to be a fashion designer; Grace Archer, whose clothes were tattered and whose nose was always running; Elaine Marx, who lived up the street from the school and whose father was a bookkeeper. What did you have to do to books to be called a bookkeeper, I wondered, until my father explained. And of course there were boys—among them fat Charlie LeValley, whose father was a plumber with LEVALLEY PLUMBING in big fat letters on his truck, and cute, towheaded Tommy Osborn, whom I had a crush on but who only had eyes for Carly.

Occasionally Carly or Patsy would invite me over after school to play, and I would be privy to a genuine Norman Rockwell family, with a real mother in the kitchen instead of a governess and servants. One Halloween, when I was in seventh grade, Carly asked me to stay over for trick-or-treating, an indulgence that was not allowed on The Place. Tommy and I always spent a lot of time at Woolworth's in downtown Long Branch picking out costumes and masks to wear to school for our Halloween parade and party, but knocking on doors and asking for candy was not a holiday ritual that my parents endorsed. That afternoon, I borrowed Mrs. Niles's skating outfit (dark green felt with a short, fur-trimmed twirly skirt and matching fur-trimmed hat), wore makeup for the first time in my life (another indulgence that wasn't allowed on The Place), and pranced door to door with Carly's "real" white leather figure skates slung over my shoulder. I felt as glamorous as my revered Sonja Henie, whom I idolized after recently seeing her in *Sun Valley Serenade* with handsome John Payne.

While stopping at one house in the neighborhood, Billy Pegram, a tall, blond, good-looking eighth grader, started flirting with me. It was the first time anyone of the opposite sex had paid any attention to me, and I was thrilled. Billy called me at home several times afterwards until my parents put an end to it, and when he left for boarding school the following fall I lost track of him.

At the Shrewsbury School there were two grades in every classroom except in eighth grade. There, thirteen of us were privileged to have our desks set up in the back of the auditorium where Mr. Madison, the principal, presided over us. I distinguished myself that year by writing a poem inspired by a Currier and Ives winter landscape that I had seen on a Christmas card, complete with a horse-drawn sleigh harboring "two lovers inside." My romantic nature had already taken root.

Starting off that eighth grade year, I was allowed to have dinner with my parents in the formal dining room under the pewter chandelier. Most of the time, my father was his usual distant and aloof self, but occasionally, when I shared with him that I was "stuck," he would volunteer to help me with my arithmetic homework. After the ritual of finger bowls and dessert, I would run upstairs to fetch my frustrating assignment. Sitting on the arm of my father's red leather chair, I would try to concentrate as he carefully deconstructed decimals and percentages and algebraic equations. He was a patient and thorough teacher, explaining mathematical concepts to me in everyday language. But I always had the feeling that he was more intrigued with the subject at hand than he actually was with me.

Nevertheless, it seems that when I need information, or when he has something to impart, he makes himself available to me. Today on the porch—before lunch is announced by our downstairs maid Val (Margaret's replacement)—I listen to his words and nod my head. I'm not sure why my father enjoys sharing his thoughts with me on the Jewish and Christian religions. Maybe he can't discuss these controversial matters with his friends and relatives, or even with my mother, a self-proclaimed atheist. Maybe he's comfortable knowing that I'm a captive audience and won't talk back or argue with him; he never questions me in regard to my personal feelings about these matters. But today is the first time that he has actually charged me to actively pursue his theories.

Despite his mixed feelings about Judaism, he attends services twice a year in the fall, on Rosh Hashanah and Yom Kippur, in New York City at Temple Emmanuel, the largest Reform synagogue in the world. My mother, despite her lack of faith, dutifully accompanies him, but I have never been asked to join them, so have had no exposure whatsoever to the faith of my forefathers.

I'm aware that the summer people—our friends who come down from New York City to the North Jersey Shore—are, like us, wealthy Reform Jews of German descent. The Ocean Beach Club and the Hollywood Golf Club that we all belong to are Jewish clubs. These people, however, don't seem particularly religious to me. At the Shrewsbury School, Elaine Marx is the only other Jew in my grade—but I don't feel any special affinity for her. I find all my Gentile classmates there much more appealing.

I'm also aware that my parents participate not only in their inherited social world of wealthy Reform Jews, but also in another new—for them—social milieu. Through ongoing friendships with my father's Princeton classmates, and various trips my parents take—in February to a Florida resort and during the summer to New England—they have developed a network of Gentile friends. This world is entirely unrelated to their Jewish crowd and seems to mean a great deal to them.

And there's something else. We are of German ancestry, which seems to be very important to my mother and father. "I can't believe they're letting in those Russian Jews," I heard my mother comment on the membership of the clubs that we belong to. "They made all their money during the war," she followed up condescendingly. It seems that there are different kinds of Jews, some more acceptable to my parents than others, and that recently acquired wealth is not as respectable as old wealth. And, it also seems, my parents think they're better than the Jews from Eastern Europe. My mother and father, I conclude, are snobs.

It's clear to me that my father has ambivalent feelings about the Jewish religion and takes no pride in being a Jew. I don't tell him that my own Jewishness is a very confusing issue for me. Perhaps he already suspects this, since he seems to be indirectly inviting me to share in his conflicts. Strangely, he never cautions me about anti-Semitism; he never warns me that I may run into prejudice during my years in boarding school and college (as he did). But I already sense from him that being Jewish means being different, and also means being segregated in certain ways, and I'm not at all comfortable with it.

Encouraging me to explore and even adopt a Christian faith, I believe he is releasing me to pursue what he feels isn't appropriate for a member of his own generation—to be disloyal to his heritage. Perhaps he feels that post-war society is more flexible and accepting of this crossing over; he doesn't elaborate.

But even if I choose another faith—as he is suggesting—I'm still a Jew. The problem is: I know that I'm Jewish; I can't deny that I'm Jewish. But how can I explain that I don't feel Jewish and don't even want to be Jewish?

It's already a dilemma for me, a fourteen-year-old girl about to leave home for the first time. For my fifty-three-year-old father—a man of the world—it's apparently still a dilemma, ongoing and unresolved.

*

After my mother's tearful goodbye in the Main Hall of the Residence on the first day of boarding school, I scampered up the wide stairway to my room on the fourth floor—eager to unpack and embark on a brand new chapter of my life. Standing in front of my bureau, putting away my underwear and socks, I looked across the hall and saw a tall, pretty, curly-haired brunette putting away *her* socks and underwear in *her* bureau—Ann, from East Hampton, Long Island—my first friend at The Baldwin School. (Fifty-seven years later, we will co-chair our 50th Reunion at Smith College).

I was assigned to a small single room connected by a doorway to a larger room with two twin beds. Later that afternoon, I met my two suitemates, Jane from Hagerstown, Maryland, and Margaret from Chattanooga, Tennessee. After lights out later that night (promptly at ten o'clock with no talking allowed afterwards), they invited me to visit. We huddled on one of the beds, whispering to each other so that Mrs. Beach, the housemother on our floor, wouldn't hear us and reprimand us. I was eager to get to know these two girls; I was all ears.

"My mother told me that I could tell the Catholic girls, because they have one eye bigger than the other," Margaret shared in hushed tones.

"My mother told me to watch out for the Jewish girls," Jane offered.

I said nothing. The room became deadly quiet. Then Jane spoke up first.

"Well, guess what! I'm Catholic!"

More dead silence. It's now or never, I thought.

"And guess what! I'm Jewish!" Another dead silence. Then the three of us burst out laughing. Our giggles were interrupted by Mrs. Beach's warning tap on the door. "No talking after lights out, girls!" she barked. I tiptoed back to my bed, and from then on, behind her back, we always referred to her as Mrs. Bitch.

CHAPTER EIGHT

School Days

———

Bells, Bells, Bells. The bells rang all day long at The Baldwin School in Bryn Mawr, Pennsylvania. There was a bell for breakfast, lunch and dinner; a bell for assembly before classes started every weekday morning; a bell for study hall before and after dinner; and of course, bells at the beginning and end of every class. Life at Baldwin, it seemed, was even more strict and regulated than it had been on The Place, but I loved everything about it.

I loved the rambling, old Victorian building known as The Residence—with its turrets and balconies and porches—that had once been the Bryn Mawr Hotel. I loved the circular driveway that led up to The Residence, lined with weeping cherry trees that bloomed every May—just before school ended—in celebratory clouds of pink blossoms. I loved the sense of community at the school; loved that we all wore the same uniforms—simple cotton dresses in pastel shades; loved that we met every weekday morning in the Assembly Room off the Main Hall—the seniors on the stage in their newly acquired blazers facing the rest of us —to stand and salute the flag, to sit for our headmistress Miss Cross's Bible reading and prayer, to listen to special announcements and a rundown of the events of the day ahead by the senior Head of Student Government. I loved walking into the quaint village of Bryn Mawr after classes with friends for hamburgers and milkshakes. I loved being allowed on weekends to take the train—the Paoli Local—into Philadelphia to explore museums and shops. And I loved the bus trips to the Academy of Music—sometimes even on school nights—to hear Eugene Ormandy conducting the Philadelphia Orchestra, or to watch the

Ballets Russes de Monte Carlo. Nothing like this was ever available to me on The Place.

Often the homework was arduous and seemed endless; we were being prepared for the top women's colleges in the country. Many of the girls—both boarding and day students—hated the workload and the restrictive rules. A number of boarders were homesick for their parents and siblings, since we were allowed only a few weekends each semester away from the campus. I, on the other hand, discovered not only privileges that didn't exist on the Place but also a fascinating new family—over two hundred girls from all over the country and a few from across the world.

The matriarch of this family—our headmistress Miss Rosamund Cross—was a tweedy woman in her late thirties with curly reddish-blond hair, china-blue eyes and an engaging smile. Rumor had it that her fiancé, a member of the Royal Canadian Air Force, had been shot down over Germany and killed during the war. She lived in a charming apartment on the ground floor of the Residence, and made a point of getting to know every one of her charges. She ran the school with velvet gloves, but I sensed that she had a will of iron. She was very spiritual and also very democratic, and although I hardly knew her, I had great respect for her. She exemplified, for me, the Christian values that my father had extolled.

I was fourteen years old, and suddenly I had a new family, a new parental figure whom I respected and admired, new challenges in the classroom and new cultural opportunities in the outside world. At Baldwin I was no longer lonely. And yes, I still loved the smell of school.

*

During my sophomore and junior years at Baldwin, I worked hard to maintain an academic average that kept me on the Honor Roll. I also followed my father's dictate, attending Sunday morning services with various classmates at the nearby Episcopal and Presbyterian churches. As I sat in the midst of these devoted congregations—totally unfamiliar with the order of the service, the rituals, the prayers and the hymns—my old feelings of being different, of not belonging, would sweep over me again. These were the only times during my four years at the school that I felt like an outsider. I learned more about the Christian faith from Miss Cross's morning assembly readings from the Old and New Testaments, and also from the homilies she delivered during our brief Sunday evening chapel service in the Assembly Room before dinner, than I did from the Sunday morning church services that I attended.

There were very few Jewish girls at Baldwin—only three others in my class of sixty-six and a few in the other grades. Miss Cross's tolerant attitudes would not allow any overt prejudice. I had surmised, however, during my three years at the school, that new Jewish boarders were always assigned single rooms—as I had been. Parents did not want to hear on the phone or by mail that their daughters had been assigned a Jewish roommate upon arriving at this prestigious school on the Main Line of Philadelphia. Anti-Semitism was very subtle at The Baldwin School.

*

The headline of *The Hourglass*, our weekly newspaper, read in bold: "JOAN COWEN ELECTED HEAD OF STUDENT GOVERNMENT." It was May of junior year, the cherry trees were in blossom, and—for the first time in my life—I knew what it meant to be popular and in demand. Since freshman year, I had grown two inches and slimmed down. The plump, shy, self-conscious fourteen-year-old from The Place had been gradually replaced by a tall, striking, confident seventeen-year-old with—as my mother would say—sex appeal. (She categorized my girl friends as either having or not having sex appeal). I had campaigned against four of my classmates, and

I had won the election. It was a heady time. That summer on The Place, boys started calling me on the phone for dates, and my parents and I started arguing about curfews.

When I returned in the fall, it was my turn to sit proudly on the stage in the front row of the Assembly Room with my sixty-five senior classmates. In my pastel cotton uniform and green Baldwin senior blazer—a large, elaborate "B" embroidered on the upper left-hand pocket—I ran each weekday morning assembly meeting with Miss Cross. Any lingering conflicts about my Jewishness and about feeling different had receded since my election and ensuing popularity. I had also started walking to Quaker Meeting on Sunday mornings in the nearby town of Haverford, where I could blend in for an hour of meditation in the eighteenth-century stone meetinghouse, and not feel like an outsider.

On the first day of school senior year, I met privately with Miss Cross in her office in The Schoolhouse—the stone building adjacent to The Residence where classes were held—to review our plans for the next two semesters. I would be meeting with her alone once a week until graduation the following June, taking her thoughts and ideas back to the Advisory Board—a group of fifteen elected students, presided over by me, who formulated and improved the regulations and privileges of the school and dealt with any infringements of these regulations and privileges. I, in turn, would take our thoughts and ideas back to her.

"Before we start, Joan, I want to share something with you," she said, in a serious, reproachful tone that scared me.

"Last spring, after you were elected, I got the impression that you were running a popularity contest. I hope you've given that up. We have serious work to do together."

My eyes welled up with tears. Miss Cross was right. Winning the election had initially gone to my head. But over the summer I had settled down, with time to think seriously about what I wanted to give back to the school during my two-semester tenure as Head of Student Government. I had campaigned on a promise to rewrite and simplify the archaic *Book of Rules and Regulations*. I wanted to make the school a warmer, friendlier place. I wanted to help people. And above all, I wanted to be fair. I shared my goals with Miss Cross, and we got down to the business of running The Baldwin School.

*

Miss Cross represented the Faculty and the Board of Trustees; I represented my Advisory Board and the student body. I loved my job as Chairman of the Advisory Board. I soon learned that I was not only good at organizing things and attending to details, but also adept at designating responsibilities to others. I loved being in a leadership position and being known and looked up to by every student in the school. I felt valuable and important.

For many years, two separate awards had been given each spring to two seniors: The White Blazer Award to the outstanding athlete, and the Dorothy Shipley Rosenmiller Award to the outstanding student who had done the most for the school. Inevitably, the Head of Student Government received this award; I was looking forward to being the chosen one. However, it was Miss Cross's intention for the Advisory Board to review the two awards, and with the help of the entire school, to improve them. She was not sure that choosing one winner for each award over several equally strong candidates was truly fair.

Together with my Advisory Board, we devised a survey and set out to interview each girl in the school, collecting criticism and also suggestions for new plans for the awards. This gave each individual student a sense of responsibility and a say in the student government, another of Miss Cross's goals for the year. That spring of senior year, for the first time in the history of the school, several girls, instead of only one, were the recipients of each award. I shared the honor with four other classmates. Secretly, I was very disappointed; it wasn't the same as being the single, outstanding winner. I had hoped to be the only one called up on the stage for the Rosenmiller Award, with everyone in the audience applauding. It would have been my swan song, my final star turn. But I knew in my heart that it was all for the best for The Baldwin School.

*

One month before graduation, our senior yearbooks were published and distributed. Miss Cross wrote in her dedication:

To the Class of 1950

As you look back upon your Senior year, I hope that you realize what you have done for the school. Morale is made up of "a lot of little things." It is because you have cared about the little things, have thought them important, that your leadership has created such a fine spirit in the school. In our world there are no longer any intimate boundaries. Crises, wars, A-bombs, and alarms are of such vast magnitude that the individual seems insignificant.

To believe this, however, is to promote your own destruction and that of others. Only if each person in every relationship is as "Right" in his action and thinking as he can possibly be, shall we be able to create a reasonable world in which to live. The right means will develop the right ends. I hope that your experience in school this year will make you leaders of citizens in your community to build this kind of morale.

Rosamund Cross

One week before graduation, I met with Miss Cross for the last time. I had taken my job as Head of Student Government very seriously; we had accomplished a lot.

But the work had consumed my days, and along with serious struggles in Basic Chemistry my marks had suffered. I would not graduate on the Honor Roll.

Miss Cross looked across her desk at me. Her china-blue eyes twinkled behind her horn-rimmed glasses.

"Joan, you'll have plenty of time at Smith next year to concentrate on your studies. Today I want to congratulate you. You're not the same person who sat here last September when we started the school year. You've grown. You've become more thoughtful, more sensitive to other people's feelings. You've learned to be a good listener. I can see it in your eyes. I'm very proud of you, Joan."

Once again, my eyes welled up with tears, this time with the joy of a job well done.

*

A few days later, on the last Sunday before graduation, one of my classmates came up to me at dinner and asked if we could meet afterwards in the Main Hall. I didn't know Iris very well, but I was aware that she spent a lot of time consulting privately with Miss Cross. I was also aware that she had a very intense relationship with her boyfriend, Buddy. When he came to visit on weekends, they were always huddled in a corner of the Main Hall, holding hands and whispering.

"I need to talk in private," she said. "Let's go for a walk."

We went outside. It was a lovely spring evening; the weeping cherry trees lining the circular driveway had burst into leaf; my year of hard work was almost over. Our long white graduation dresses— carefully picked out while home at Easter time—were hanging upstairs in our closets. Sixty-six of us would be graduating in a few days; thirteen of us, including myself, would be going on to Smith College in the fall.

We walked in tandem down the driveway, inhaling the balmy air, when suddenly Iris burst out, "I don't know what to do!" Then she started to sob. "Miss Cross is going to kill me! After all her extra help! I'll be kicked out of school, just at the end!"

"What's the matter? Get hold of yourself and tell me!"

She stopped sobbing, took a deep breath, then said calmly,

"Buddy and I eloped ... we got married secretly over Easter vacation."

My mind was racing. How could I let Iris sabotage all *her* years of hard work at The Baldwin School out of loyalty to Miss Cross? It was all too much to bear. We paced up and down the driveway as I searched for a solution. I thought of my father, whose moral principles I admired, and wondered what he would say if he were in my place. I continued to pace and ponder for a minute or two with my distraught classmate still sniffling at my side; then I made my decision.

"Iris, we're going back inside and nobody—I mean NOBODY—is ever going to know about this conversation."

*

Rumors were flying that last week of school. One of our classmates, Abby, a very sophisticated day student from Bryn Mawr who sometimes boarded with us when her parents traveled, had broken a series of rules and was in serious trouble. None of us was certain what she had done to enrage Miss Cross; we imagined it had to do with her boyfriend, a Yale senior—an "older man" in our innocent eyes. Smoking and drinking were also involved, we suspected. We, the Advisory Board, were waiting to be called on to inflict punishment for her misdemeanors. I had resolved not to be too harsh or severe, and I knew my classmates on the Board would follow my example.

Five days before graduation, Miss Cross called an emergency meeting after dinner in her apartment on the ground floor of the Residence, ostensibly to discuss Abby's predicament. She had a stony look on her face.

"Abby has not only broken the rules, but she has also lied to me. I am taking this matter into my own hands. She will not be allowed to attend graduation on Friday—she will not march or sit with the class. That is all I have to say."

She got up and left the room. I was stunned and shattered. I had saved Iris from Miss Cross's wrath, but Abby's Baldwin years were ruined; I had not been able to help her. On the way upstairs with my friend Ann from East Hampton, the Secretary of the Advisory Board, who was also going off to Smith, I burst out crying.

"I don't need any more of this shit! Screw student government! Screw trying to help people! When I get to Smith I'm just going to do my homework and have a good time! "

Abby had been a day student since kindergarten; I suspected she and Miss Cross shared a prior history of misdemeanors that I didn't know about. But I was overcome by the cruelty—and the timing—of the punishment. Why couldn't I and my Advisory Board decide what was "Right?" At the very least, why couldn't we have a say in the proceedings, even if Miss Cross might ultimately choose to override us? Where was the mercy and forgiveness that she had exemplified for me over the past four years? I felt humiliated and betrayed by a woman I had so respected and admired.

Graduation Day dawned sunny and clear—a glorious June morning for the ceremony. Sixty-five of us marched through the Gothic arches of Goodhart Hall on the Bryn Mawr College campus across the street from The Residence, resplendent in our long white dresses, each carrying a huge bouquet of white roses. My parents, my Aunt Virginia, my brother Tommy, even Mamzelle were all on hand. I was smiling on the outside, proud of my accomplishments, but a piece of my heart was heavy. My glory year had ended on a bittersweet note.

CHAPTER NINE
Troubles

S ix hundred five of us arrived on the Smith College campus in
Northampton, Massachusetts in September of 1950—fresh-
faced, dewy-eyed and virginal. At least most of us were virgins, I assumed. Sex before marriage for young women was frowned
upon in those days; virginity was prized; and as far as I knew, sexual activity or lack of it, was not openly discussed among most of us.
Born in the early 1930s during the Great Depression, we were not
rebellious; we did what we were told and spoke when we were spoken to. Sociologists had already dubbed us "The Silent Generation."
We had also grown up as the last generation without television; in
1950, only nine percent of American homes possessed a TV set.

The Smith College Class of 1954 was predominantly Protestant;
some members were Catholic, some Jewish, but only three were
"colored," as members of the Negro race were referred to back then.
"Black" and "African-American" were terms that had not yet entered
our vocabulary. No one of Asian heritage was represented in our class.

Before I left for Northampton my father had given me another
one of his mini-lectures.

"Joan, you're going to meet all kinds of Jews in your life. But I
want you to remember something. There are Jews like us, and there
are kikes. We are not kikes."

It was an ugly word—a word I had never heard before. I wasn't
really sure what he meant, but he was right about meeting all kinds
of Jews when I got to Smith College. There were wealthy Jewish
girls from godless households who had attended private schools—
like me. There were loud, brassy, self-confident Jewish girls from
public high schools who all seemed to know each other. There were

quiet Jewish girls from very observant families who belonged to Hillel, the center for Jewish life on campus, and celebrated more religious holidays than I had ever heard of. There were Jewish girls on scholarship who had grown up in Brooklyn or Jersey City over their parents' shops and stores. But I was still in spiritual limbo, and I still felt different from all of them. Although I still didn't feel Jewish and I still didn't want to be Jewish, I was too honest to try and "pass" by denying my heritage.

Freshman year found me on a fourth floor again—this time with five other classmates (each one of us in an identical single room) in Laura Scales House, a handsome brick dormitory in the Quadrangle—a newer part of campus where Commencement was always held outdoors in June. I represented New Jersey, Talia (short for Natalia) and Mildred (dubbed Mud by a senior the first day of school) represented Connecticut, Julie was from Kansas, and the two Janes were from, respectively, Ohio and Massachusetts. (There were twenty-three freshmen in the house, along with fifty upper-classmen.) I don't know who chose the six of us to be together or why, but Mud was the token Catholic, I was the token Jew.

After the experience with my two suitemates on my first night at Baldwin, I didn't want to be ambushed by any anti-Semitic remarks at Smith. Late one afternoon, early in the semester, I decided to confide in one of my new fourth floor friends, Jane from Massachusetts—who lived next door—assuming she would spread the word.

"There's something I want you to know—I'm Jewish." I blurted out. Jane nodded her head. Maybe she already knew; she didn't comment.

Recalling my father's words, I then added, "My father says there are Jews like us and then there are kikes."

The words had an ugly thud. But Jane only nodded her head once more. We went downstairs together for dinner, and the subject never came up again.

A week or so later, I was talking to Talia about our "big sisters"—as freshmen we were each assigned an upperclassman in our dormitory whom we could turn to for advice with whatever problems we encountered during our first year on campus. I had been given a very preppy, flighty sophomore from New Jersey who had completely ignored me since we met the first day of the semester. She had attended the same boarding school as Talia before entering Smith.

"I guess she thinks I don't need any help—after four years of boarding school," I told Talia.

Talia shook her head. "I can tell you why she's been ignoring you," she confided. "She complained to me a few weeks ago, 'They had to give me a Jew.'"

Anti-Semitism was alive and well at Smith College in the fall of 1950.

*

After the academic rigors of The Baldwin School, I found the course work easy that first year of college. Freshman English and French were no more demanding than my classes had been at Baldwin; European History, a large lecture class, was not my favorite but I could handle it. I had come to Smith as a potential music major after twelve years studying classical piano. But I soon discovered that the required composition classes were arduous, and that I hated the solitary practice hours I was expected to put in on the piano. I played "nicely," but I was certainly not concert pianist material, and I was too shy and self-conscious to sit down at the baby grand in the living room of our dorm to play spontaneously for my housemates. I gave up the piano, but had no idea what my concentration would be. By sophomore year I hoped that one of my lecture courses would trigger a passionate, sustainable interest.

By then the six of us from the fourth floor had moved downstairs and taken over the far end of the second floor, incorporating into our clique a few other girls with whom we had become friendly. I loved all my friends, and I certainly didn't think we were any more boisterous and irreverent than the other two thousand members of the Silent Generation on campus. But a recent addition to our gang, Barbara (a.k.a. BooBoo) from Milwaukee, was definitely more high-spirited and iconoclastic than the rest of us. BooBoo was engaged to a Navy veteran who was getting his engineering degree at Yale; he had transferred from Northwestern our sophomore year to be closer to Smith, and also to keep tabs on BooBoo (she had had an intense romance freshman year with Massachusetts Jane's older brother, also a war veteran.)

BooBoo was with us from Monday through Friday for classes on campus and meals in the house, spending almost every weekend in New Haven with her husband-to-be. Cars were forbidden until the second semester of senior year, but BooBoo kept her fiancé's car secretly parked on a side street near the dormitory, for quick getaways to New Haven.

During the week at dinnertime, our housemother Mrs. Chandler, a dour widow whom we had nicknamed The Chan, expected silence while she pronounced grace—a tradition at the evening meal. One evening, when she was going on longer than usual, BooBoo whispered loudly from our table in the back of the dining room, "For Christ's sake, let's eat!" Everyone burst out laughing, bringing an abrupt end to our housemother's incantations.

As sophomore year wore on, The Chan started referring to our group as "that Rowdy Crew" on the second floor—a nickname that has continued to stick with us. BooBoo dropped out at the end of that year to get married in Milwaukee over the summer; several members of The Rowdy Crew were in attendance as bridesmaids. I'm certain that—no matter how well-behaved or raucous the rest of us were during our remaining two years at Smith—BooBoo's extreme rowdiness had set the tone and sealed our moniker in Mrs. Chandler's (and our) vocabulary forever.

That second year at Smith, I had given up my music courses and was living up to the vow I had made to Ann on the staircase at Baldwin a few days before graduation. I was studying hard, dating various young men and avoiding any extracurricular activities. An Art History survey course really intrigued me and could have led to a major, but lecture courses as a whole really bored me. I was also intrigued with the idea of a Junior Year Abroad in Paris—since, thanks to Mamzelle's efforts, I was quite fluent in French—but my parents would not endorse it. I'm sure they were worried that I would be preyed upon by a lascivious Frenchman and get into all sorts of trouble; little did they realize that there was plenty of trouble lurking in Western Massachusetts.

Hoping that small seminars and one-on-one conferences with professors would be more intellectually challenging, at the end of sophomore year I applied and was accepted into the English Honors program. I embarked first semester of junior year on a stimulating seminar with Daniel Aaron, a middle-aged, renowned Harvard-educated professor who specialized in nineteenth century American Literature. We started off with Poe, Hawthorne, Melville and Twain, but when Henry James was introduced after Christmas vacation, I had found my master. I wrote my term paper at the end of the semester on James, and later on, in the spring, asked Mr. Aaron if he would be my thesis advisor on James senior year. He not only accepted but also asked me to stay on in Northampton over the summer to help him with a research project he was working on for a projected book.

My housemates were impressed and thrilled for me. When I went home for spring vacation and mentioned it to my parents at dinner, the response was immediate and unambiguous. "Absolutely out of the question," pronounced my father from his end of the mahogany table under the pewter chandelier; my mother nodded her head in agreement from the other end.

I hadn't attached any personal feelings to Mr. Aaron; he was my teacher, an older man at least twenty years my senior. I could not have cared less if he was gay or straight, single or a family man. If anything, I was in awe of him. But I'm sure my parents thought he was planning a seduction. Their unequivocal "no" ended whatever kind of research I would have pursued with Daniel Aaron over the summer of 1953 in Northampton.

During that spring of junior year, my classmate Carol, a member of The Rowdy Crew, arranged a blind date for me through the Amherst man she was dating. Derrik Cutten Hoitsma was tall and athletically built—a good-looking guy with china blue eyes and a strawberry blond crew cut that accounted for his nickname Red. His background couldn't have been more different from mine, which intrigued me. His maternal grandfather, George Barton Cutten, a Baptist minister from Nova Scotia, had been president of Colgate University from 1922 to 1942; his mother Muriel Cutten had grown up on the campus where she had met and married Red's father, Ralph Hoitsma, a Colgate student from Wyoming. Red had been raised in Shaker Heights, a suburb of Cleveland, Ohio, where he had attended public high school before coming east to college.

I admired Red's energy and drive; we had fun together, and continued dating during the fall and into the winter of senior year. Red and his Amherst friends and their dates from Smith and Mt. Holyoke were a pleasant diversion for me from the demands of the Honors Program and my ongoing thesis deadlines. We were drinking buddies, tentatively experimenting with sex. It was a typical college romance; I really didn't think it was going anywhere.

In early February, I went on another blind date with a teacher from the Deerfield School, a highly regarded boys' boarding school not far from Northampton. In his early thirties, Brad was a veteran of the Korean War; he was teaching English and Math at Deerfield and seemed ever so worldly and sophisticated to me, especially compared to the college boys I had been dating since freshman year. I was completely infatuated with him, and judging from the clever homemade Valentine he sent me, he must have been smitten, too. Red was going to Florida with some of his Amherst classmates for spring vacation, and when Brad invited me to visit him at Deerfield, while the school was closed for spring vacation, I was thrilled. The weekend, however, turned into a disaster, when I realized that he not only had a serious drinking problem but also expected me to enter into a full-blown affair with him. I headed back to New Jersey for the remainder of vacation, where my parents were fraught with worry; I had neglected to tell them how they could get in touch with me, and, as usual, they were imagining worst-case scenarios. I waited for Red to pick me up and drive me to Northampton on his way back from Florida. With only two months left before graduation, it was easy to fall back into our "safe" relationship, which included drinking and occasional heavy petting, but nothing threatening compared to Brad's frightening ways.

*

In the 1950s, few of us women were actually encouraged to undertake serious careers, which may have accounted for our somewhat cavalier attitude towards our educations. It was gently implied that marriage was our mission; we joked that we were at Smith to get our MRS Degree along with our BA. My close friend Barb, from Providence, had spent her junior year in Geneva. She was a political science major, and when she went home for Christmas vacation senior year asked her father if she could apply to law school. "What? Are you crazy?" He responded. "I just spent a fortune on your education at Smith, and I have your brother and sister coming up!" A year later, Barb fell in love with a young Australian businessman—

the son of a business associate of her father's from down under who had come to Providence to work briefly for his company. She married and moved to Melbourne for the rest of her life.

Another housemate, Nancy from New Haven, was also taking English Honors, and we shared a number of seminars together. I was bright, as were most of my close friends in The Rowdy Crew, but Nancy was brilliant. I was bowled over by her intellect. When she was elected to Phi Beta Kappa and called home to tell her parents the thrilling news, her mother answered the phone. "I think she would have been happier if I'd called to tell her I was engaged," Nancy confided in me.

Looking back, I'm convinced that had we been born ten years later, our high spirits and repressed rebelliousness would have been channeled into the Women's Movement. In 1963, author Betty Friedan, a Smith 1942 graduate, kicked off the movement with the publication of *The Feminine Mystique*, her explosive critique of middle-class patterns which helped millions of women articulate a pervasive sense of discontent. She argued that women often had no outlets for expression other than finding a husband and bearing children—a role defined by generations of male-dominated society. Her groundbreaking philosophy was aided and abetted by the emergence of the sexual revolution of the 1960s. The Rowdy Crew, however, was not prescient, and certainly not ready in the early 1950s to embrace the new roles and responsibilities—both personal and professional—that Friedan would encourage a decade later.

By spring of senior year I was finishing up my thesis and also taking a poetry seminar with Elizabeth Drew, an authority on T. S. Eliot. Janet, from New York City, one of my classmates in the seminar, decided—with the approval of the professor in charge of the Honors Program and the enthusiasm of all of us enrolled in English Honors—to host a cocktail party for the entire English Department, both full professors and instructors, at the Faculty House. She designed the invitation, choosing a sprightly quote by Ogden Nash to be printed on its cover:

Candy is dandy, but liquor is quicker.

During the party, which turned out to be a huge success, the head of the English department (whose daughter happened to be a classmate) took Janet aside and asked her who had written the invitations. She acknowledged that she was an admirer of Nash's work and had designed them.

"Did you stop and think of the implications of the Ogden Nash quote?" he went on to ask her in a serious, critical tone.

Janet, expecting a compliment on her creativity, was taken aback. "What do you mean?" she asked.

"Well," he responded in a pontifical voice, familiar to us from his lectures, "If a young man brings a box of candy to a young woman, that's one thing. If he brings liquor, that's quite something else."

Janet had thought the quote was catchy and witty, and told me she was too naïve to have considered its sexual implications. No one else in the English Department complained about it, but the incident epitomized the morality that many of our elders had handed down to any number of us in the 1950s—sex was mysterious, threatening and forbidden, and men were not to be trusted (especially if they plied you with liquor). In my own life, Brad was certainly a living example of their worst fears.

Unlike Janet, who admitted to being studious and naïve and to having led a very sheltered life, I was considered lively and sophisticated by my classmates. After all, thanks to my parents' expertise, I knew my way around Manhattan and was familiar with all the theaters, shops, and good restaurants. I had dined and danced at the Stork Club (more than once), could talk my way through an elaborate French menu (*en français, bien sûr*), and knew how to order (and sip) an extra dry gin martini. But Smith College was a big, cold, competitive place, and I never quite found myself there. I missed the family feeling and the mentorship of Miss Cross that had sustained me during my four years in Bryn Mawr. Looking back, I should have overcome my sudden disenchantment with student government and helping other people that last week at Baldwin, when Iris confided in me and Abby was not allowed to graduate. I should have rebounded and pursued a leadership role on the Smith campus—similar to the one in which I had excelled throughout my senior year at Baldwin—a role that had brought out the best in me. Instead I got on the wrong track, and I wasn't feeling good about myself.

Something essential was missing for me at Smith—and more importantly missing in me—that prevented me from finding joy and inspiration in my accomplishments and my day-to-day life there. My parents' lack of interest in and enthusiasm for some of my dreams certainly didn't help. In any case, during my junior and senior years, even though I seemed outwardly happy and busy with studying and dating, inwardly I was becoming more and more lonely and depressed. I was getting through, but I had lost my rudder. I was seriously troubled—and I was setting myself up for more troubles ahead.

CHAPTER TEN

Cum Laude

O n a clear, shining morning in early June 1954, we marched into the Quadrangle, capped and gowned in traditional black. Our proud parents sat attentively in white folding chairs, row-on-row, contemplating the pasts and futures of their daughters. For four ongoing years they had invested almost two thousand dollars a year—the price of a Plymouth or Chevrolet—in our college educations.

Four hundred sixty-one of us were receiving our diplomas. This attrition rate of almost twenty-five percent (since opening day of freshman year) was not surprising. Some classmates had dropped out to get married or to transfer to other colleges, others because of serious illness, family problems, or unexpected pregnancies. (The "pill" was not released until 1960; abortion was not legalized until 1973.) Many of those graduating were already engaged, proudly sporting diamond rings; they had been planning their post-commencement weddings throughout senior year.

We were thrilled to have Alistair Cooke as our commencement speaker—flattered that he had agreed to speak at a "girls' school," albeit the largest women's college in the world. Born in Manchester, England in 1908, the son of a tradesman, Cooke had attended Cambridge University on a scholarship. He had come to the United States in 1932 to study theater at Yale and then Harvard. Elegant, erudite, and witty, Cooke was well known to all of us—graduates and parents alike—for his radio and television broadcasts here and for his admiration of all things American. He had become an American citizen in 1941 just before the outbreak of World War II.

The United States had emerged from the War as the most powerful country in the world, and despite an uneasy truce in Korea, an unshakeable spirit of optimism was spreading across America. General Dwight Eisenhower, who had organized and led the conquest of Western Europe, had been elected to the Presidency in 1952. "Ike's" warmth, sincerity and humility, coupled with his awesome heroism, were inspiring. The economy was booming; television and commercial aviation were shrinking the globe.

In Northampton, Massachusetts, on that sunny June morning in the Quad, surrounded by Georgian brick dormitories and graceful archways and ivy-covered walls, jubilation was in the air.

Cooke started off his commencement address with his familiar charm and humor. He wished each one of us "a happy marriage ... the supreme role that all of you will hanker after, even the art students and sociologists among you ... far and away the most important thing that can happen to you." He told us that "fate has already started to weave a web of romance and insurance policies and diapers around many of you," and that our fortunes were already being decided at that moment by "anonymous young men ... in New Haven, in Cambridge, in Williamstown, in Princeton ... even perhaps in Grinnell, Iowa, or Berkeley, California." In the meantime, he suggested, "As you leave these surroundings and return to your homes, I can recommend no career more urgent or challenging for a little while to come than the career of tolerating your parents. If this career becomes irksome, you can console yourselves with the reflection that it will soon give way to the more challenging occupation of tolerating your children."

Everyone found this droll and amusing, but halfway through his speech, Cooke suddenly shifted to a somber tone, launching into "our place in history." He described the first half of the twentieth century as being "an age of unparalleled barbarism and violence," reminding us that our country was, for the first time in history, the supreme power on this earth in a world that "half-distrusts and half-hates us." Then he charged us with the awesome and painful task of trying to "repair and fortify Western civilization." He told us that nations—and individuals—can best negotiate from strength when they know well their own weaknesses:

> We cannot wish that other nations become like us ... We must prove that the liberty of other peoples, and dependent peoples, is as precious as our own; we have to learn that real friendship springs from the awareness of differences and the respect for them ... You will have to be more sensitive, less patronizing to the feelings of other peoples, than any previous generation of Americans. If you are not, you will be hated.

Cooke was not clairvoyant; he knew from experience what he was talking about. He understood the arrogance and tyranny of imperialism; he had seen his native country pass through its own glory. Having witnessed the decline of the British Empire, he was trying to warn us of the pitfalls of power. The publishing house Knopf thought so much of Cooke's history lesson that they published his entire commencement address in a slim, handsome volume later that year. My parents purchased a small stack of them to hand out to friends.

But on that gorgeous spring morning in June of 1954, in that picture-perfect setting on the campus of the largest women's college in the world, I wasn't laughing with everyone else at Cooke's witty words, nor was I spellbound by his history lesson. Surrounded by my happy, excited classmates, with my parents, my brother Tommy and my boyfriend Red sitting nearby, all smiling at me across the aisle, I should have been euphoric; after all my hard work I was graduating with honors—*cum laude* (with praise). Instead I was having trouble concentrating and sharing the excitement, worried to death that I was four weeks pregnant.

A month before, on a Saturday morning in early May, Red—now a senior at Amherst—had picked me up in his car in Northampton; we then drove to Hanover for Dartmouth Houseparty Weekend.

Like many of my classmates, I had held on to my virginity through-out my four college years. But there was a lot of fumbling around in bed after a very late Saturday night of drinking; I knew it was a dangerous time of the month for me.

Even though we had dated on and off for over a year, I certain-ly didn't think of the two of us as soulmates for life. We were still drinking together, still tentatively experimenting with sex—a pair of twenty-one-year-olds clinging to one another, both terrified of the great abyss that loomed ahead of us after commencement. We partied that spring semester—letting of steam as we finished up final exams and papers.

Red planned to start a career in Wall Street immediately after his graduation from Amherst; my father had arranged for a summer internship at a small firm headed up by one of his many business acquaintances. He was also awaiting orders to report to the U.S. Air Force for flight training; military duty for young men was still com-pulsory, and he had served in the Air Force ROTC while in college.

Following Cooke's dictate, I was returning home to The Place with my parents for the summer. They thought I showed promise as a writer, and arranged a casual meeting with a famous *Life Magazine* photographer who had married the daughter of close friends. We met in July at the Ocean Beach Club; I must have impressed him since he promised to set up an interview in September for the *Time-Life* training program. It was a rare opportunity, but I felt completely helpless and unprepared; I had no confidence in myself. My child-hood years on the estate had been far removed from the real world beyond its winding gravel driveway and stone gateposts. Since leav-ing there at age fourteen for boarding school and college, I had tried to do my best in the cloistered walls of academe, but I had never worked a day in my life. On the outside I seemed to have everything; on the inside loneliness and depression haunted me again—even more intensely, sharpened by my obsessive fears of pregnancy.

I was tall, strong and healthy that summer of 1954, but as the weeks wore on my body started to change—at first imperceptibly, especially to those around me. Throughout July and August Red and I saw each occasionally on weekends, but were rarely alone together—usually surrounded by other college friends who were also awaiting future plans. I sensed that—at least for me—the romance was waning; consumed with worry about the pregnancy, I had retreated into myself and had lost any interest in sex. But when I tried to share my concerns, Red wouldn't listen. I couldn't get his ear.

"You're just imagining things," he kept telling me, preoccupied with his demanding internship and consumed with his own personal worries about the future.

Gradually my condition became more and more obvious to me—and I worried that soon it would be obvious to others. By the end of summer I didn't know where to turn; I felt totally trapped and more terrified than ever. I was filled with despair. I thought about suicide, but couldn't imagine how to go about it without inflicting even more pain on myself. Life stretched ahead like a dark tunnel; something I had no control over was swallowing me up.

I waited until the morning in early September when Tommy drove off to Providence for his sophomore year at Brown; I did not want to involve him in the impending crisis. That afternoon, after lunch with my mother and her sister, my Aunt Virginia, I retreated upstairs to my bedroom. The big rambling house surrounded me; it seemed strangely empty and still. Outside my windows, the lawns and gardens stretched away, the tall, leafy trees tinged with the golds and russets of early autumn.

I had occupied this bedroom since the day I was born, and almost nothing in it had changed during my twenty-two years, as far as I could remember, except the wallpaper. The twin maple beds, the night tables, the highboy and the desk were old and mellow and left over from my grandparents' day. In my thirteenth year, after the War ended, I was allowed to choose a new paper. The faded Cinderella characters were torn down and replaced with butterflies and wild flowers floating on a background of pink, my favorite color at the time. That year I was also given a kidney-shaped dressing table with a white organdy skirt, topped with a mirror—now that I was old enough to wear lipstick and powder my nose, with my parents' approval.

I studied my reflection in the old full-length mirror on the outside of the bathroom door. Over the desk behind me, I could see my college diploma, neatly framed in black. In the mirror, my shiny brown penny loafers, navy blue knee socks, pleated gray flannel skirt and navy blue cashmere sweater monogrammed at the neck, were perfectly coordinated. My chestnut brown pageboy, bright pink lipstick (Revlon's Bachelor's Carnation), and large gray-green eyes (my grandmother's eyes and my best feature, I was told) completed the picture of the quintessential Smith College 1954 graduate, ready to take on the world.

But my breasts felt tender and constrained under the cashmere, and when I hiked up my sweater and examined the taut pleats hugging my hips, I noticed that I had begun to show.

I would have to go downstairs and tell her. Now.

*

I slowly walked down the first flight of the long, wide staircase. Suddenly, as I crossed the landing, I was in a frantic state—my heart pounding like a jackhammer. I saw my mother over the balcony, sitting snugly in her corner of the spacious sofa, working contently on her needlepoint until it would be time to meet my father's train. Ahead of me was the second flight of stairs. This time my father was not waiting expectantly below, smiling through the banisters, with a little white shoebox tucked under his elbow.

I sat down at the opposite end of the sofa and took a deep breath. "Mom, I have something to tell you."

My mother looked up inquisitively from her sewing, then took another stitch.

"I haven't had my period since May." My words hung in a little balloon above us.

She put down her needlepoint. Her eyes widened in shock and disbelief. "What are you trying to tell me?"

"You know. What I just said."

"I don't believe this, Joan." She caught her breath. "Are you sure?"

"Pretty sure," I lied. "What else could it be?" I was feeling desperate.

"How could you do this to me?" Her face tightened up and she started to cry.

I knew I shouldn't have told her. I should have confided in my classmate Carol earlier over the summer. She was getting married in a few weeks and was experienced with men, I was sure, although we never spoke of such matters. Her mother was young and beautiful; her stepfather was a doctor and maybe he could have helped. But Red had told me all summer I was imagining things—and I wanted to believe him.

My mother glared at me. "In my day, nice girls were virgins when they got married. I don't understand this modern generation."

Thanks, Mom. Thanks for all your faith, hope, and charity.

Her mouth turned down in a sneer. "I always suspected that behind that big brain of yours you were oversexed."

I thought back to the Houseparty weekend with Red in May—the fumblings in the dark that were totally unsatisfactory, unsatisfying, stupid.

"Well, I'm certainly not going to bother your father at the office," she continued. "We'll discuss this when he gets home in a few hours."

What a bitch she is, I thought to myself. I really hate her guts.

"In the meantime, I'll call Doug Ackerman. Thank God Harry Slater's not alive," she added with a sigh. "I couldn't drag him through this."

My mother had adored Dr. Slater; she had worshipped the ground he walked on. A surgeon and chief of staff at Monmouth Memorial Hospital, he had delivered both my brother and me and had been our family doctor for years. The walls of his office, which adjoined his house near the hospital in Long Branch, were covered with diplomas and memorabilia from his years at Princeton and Columbia Medical School. He was a tweedy, pipe-smoking country doctor with the sweetest bedside manner, beloved in the community for decades, but, of course, too tweedy, too sweet, for such matters as clandestine college sex, unwanted pregnancies, illicit abortions. When he retired, Doug Ackerman had taken over his practice. I had been to Dr. Ackerman for perfunctory school health exams, but I barely knew him.

My mother got up from the sofa and disappeared through the swinging door of the dining room into the pantry. I heard her voice murmuring into the telephone. The antique clock on the corner shelf behind me, usually benevolent and comforting, frowned down on me. Its seconds ticked away ominously; they echoed my heart—still pounding through the navy blue cashmere.

My mother returned to the living room. "Doug can see us right away." Her voice had a flat, dull sound, tinged with disapproval. I had destroyed her perfect world.

*

"Place your feet in the stirrups, dearie," directed the plump, kindly nurse as she deftly swathed my naked lower body in a sterile sheet. I still had on my knee socks; my legs poked up awkwardly from inside the sheet. When Dr. Ackerman entered the examining room the nurse came around to my side, cupping my hand in hers and massaging it gently. He spread my knees apart and I drifted into numbness—pretending I was somewhere else, hoping that this was only a bad dream, praying that it wasn't really happening to me.

"What was the date of your last period?" He asked. A sudden sharp pain delayed my answer. The nurse massaged my hand even harder as he left the room.

I got dressed and joined my mother in Dr. Ackerman's office, where he sat officiously behind his desk. My mother had a look of thorough disgust on her face.

"How could she do this to me, Doug?" Her voice trembled.

"Don't be so hard on her, Ruth," he addressed her. "She's a good girl. Actually, her hymen was still intact. And I understand he's a nice boy from a nice family." He hesitated. "But it's probably too late for me to arrange anything … " His voice melted away.

My mother sniffed and sighed. "Thanks for seeing us right away, Doug. Eddie and I will work it out when he gets home."

"Call me tomorrow. I'm here if you need to talk."

We drove back to the house in silence. As we approached the driveway she spoke in clipped tones. "You have two choices, Joan. You can go away and have the baby, and never see Red again. Or the two of you can decide to get married. Please call him and have him come down for dinner tonight after work."

Upstairs in my room I dialed Red at his workplace. "I just got back from the doctor," I said, my voice cracking up with tears. I didn't have to explain.

"Jesus." Then a pause. "Listen, Joan, everything will be fine." His voice took on a breezy tone. "Don't worry about a thing. I'll drive down right after work."

I sat down on the edge of my bed and stared at the carefree butterflies on my pink floral wallpaper. I heard the delicate tinkle of china and crystal as the table was prepared for dinner in the dining room downstairs; I heard the familiar clunk of the big, paneled front door slamming shut as my mother left for the train station. Whatever happened, whatever path I chose, I would be leaving this seemingly idyllic world behind. Life on The Place, secure and orderly, would go on, day in and day out—but nothing, for me, would ever be the same. I lay down on the bed and once again let the numbness encircle me.

Twenty minutes later I heard the front door again, followed by the metallic clank of the elevator door closing, and the predictable hum of the old Otis as it ascended to the second floor. The warped floorboards in the hallway outside my bedroom gave their usual creak. My father limped through the doorway in his handsome business suit, my mother trailing behind him. I jumped up from my bed impetuously and threw my arms around him, burying my face in the rich, dark fabric. I had never before in my life embraced him this way. I wanted to feel forever protected and comforted by him; I wanted his power to envelop me.

"Oh Daddy! I'm so sorry!" I blurted out, the tears streaming down my face.

He pushed me away gently, then crossed the room and leaned against my desk, fingering the gold pocket watch in the vest pocket of his elegant suit. I sat back down on the edge of the bed, confused and disoriented.

"Listen, Joan, these things happen." He seemed very calm, very casual. "I don't want you to be upset about it."

I was speechless, my eyes still choked with tears. How could he be so removed? Where were his feelings? I wanted him to show some emotion. If he couldn't understand and sympathize with my pain, at least he could scream out his anger and disappointment. Instead, he started reminiscing about a Princeton classmate of his.

"Chauncey Morgan's daughter had the same problem. . . . She had a beautiful wedding. . . . We got a birth announcement four months later. . . ." His voice trailed off.

I thought of all the report cards I had brought home over the years. I thought of all the accomplishments, all the achievements. Over my father's shoulder, I saw the black calligraphy of my diploma, dancing up and down, mocking me through my tears. Cum Laude. But I was tired of being perfect without praise. Didn't anybody understand? Didn't anybody really care?

"Red will be out soon. I know we can all come to a sensible solution," my father stated in a philosophical tone.

*

Over cocktails and dinner, a hasty marriage was arranged. My parents and Red actually seemed to be excited about it. I was smiling on the outside; on the inside I had climbed back into my circle of numbness. My mother and father also concocted a cover story. They would tell their friends—and we could tell our friends—that we had eloped over Spring Break and were expecting a baby around Valentine's Day. The dates would jibe perfectly.

A week later, the two of us stood together at the altar of the Little Church Around The Corner, a quaint, old, stone Episcopal Church on 29th Street in Manhattan, famous for marrying actors and actresses. I wore a dark blue silk suit—already in my wardrobe—and my gold circle pin. Both sets of parents were witnesses. The benevolent minister told me I reminded him of a beautiful stage actress from the 1930's—a name unfamiliar to me—but this was little consolation.

After a celebratory dinner with our respective parents at the Princeton Club of New York, Red and I drove to a charming inn an hour away in the town of Princeton for the weekend. The legitimate sex didn't seem any better than the fumblings around that previous May. I found it invasive, uncomfortable and messy—it was not a positive experience for me. Besides, I was worried about the baby I was carrying in my belly. Sex was definitely not my favorite thing.

Red had recently received his orders to report to Lackland Air Force Base in San Antonio for basic training in mid-September. The timing could not have been better. My father consulted with the local Ford dealer, and with Red's consent, traded in the trusty, battered gray Studebaker that had seen him through his college years for a brand new compact station wagon. On a clear, cool mid-September morning, a few days after the ceremony, we threw our suitcases in the way back and kissed my parents goodbye in the driveway.

"Safe trip! We'll see you at Christmastime ... at Christmastime!" they cried out, almost in unison, after we were settled in the front seat and ready to take off. My eyes welled up with tears. I still couldn't believe this was really happening to me. Red seemed un-perturbed. The tires of our shiny, black Ford Falcon crunched down the gravel driveway. We sailed past the spreading purple beech tree and out beyond the old stone gateposts into the real world, heading due south for San Antonio, Texas.

And that was how I left The Place.

(above) Red with Ricky and Jimmy, his brother Kin on left, at the Ocean Beach Club, August 1957.

(left) Lisa, Ricky and Jimmy at The Place, summer 1959. (Teke was born in September.)

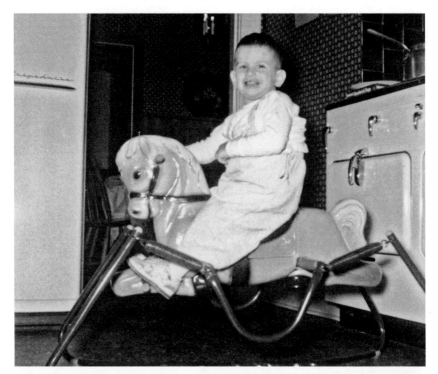

Teke, 1½ years old, winter 1961.

My parents, summer 1961.

Tommy and Connie leaving their wedding reception, the Park Lane Hotel, NYC, June 16, 1962.

Teke, Lisa, Ricky, Jimmy on The Place with baby Jennifer and Todd, 2, Tommy and Connie's children, summer 1967.

My wedding picture, taken a few weeks before my marriage to Mike Bowman.
The lace dress and pillbox hat were from Henri Bendel. September, 1967.

My wedding day,
September 16, 1967.

Lisa, 11, with Bo, 8 months old, spring 1969.

Jonathan, 2, and Bo, 5, on The Place, summer 1974.

My 4 Hoitsma hippies on The Place, Christmas Day, 1977.

Smile for the camera! Jonathan and Bo on The Place, Christmas Day, 1977.

Waiting for the ceremony to start at Derrik (a.k.a. Ricky) and Marge Pivar's wedding, Camp Mohawk in the Berkshires, June 20, 1988.

My mother's last Christmas Eve on The Place. She died February 20, 1990.

The happy couple.

The whole gang at Tommy and Connie's in Greenwich, CT. My granddaughter Sheyna, 9, (Derrik and Marge's daughter) in front row with me on left, Christmas Day, 1999.

The 6 kids with me on my 70th birthday sail, NYC, August 18, 2002.

Bo on my 70ᵗʰ birthday sail, NYC, August 18, 2002.

Lisa and Buck's engagement picture for the *New York Times*, May 2004.

Lisa at her wedding at The Boathouse in Central Park with all her siblings including Erica and Greg Hoitsma, May 2, 2004.

Pam and Jim at Lisa's wedding, May 2, 2004.　　Sheyna, sweet sixteen, 2006.

The whole gang—Bowmans, Hoitsmas, Cowens and Favorinis—in Central Park, May 2, 2004.

Receiving my MFA Degree from Sarah Lawrence College, May 20, 2005.

Bo and Andy at a wedding in Brooklyn, 2007.

My grandchildren Cruz and Pilar (Kristie and Teke's children) at home in Dallas, December 2008.

CHAPTER ELEVEN
A Sea Change

When I left for Texas in September of 1954, I had never entered the doors of a supermarket; I had never turned on a washing machine; I couldn't even boil water. I was armed with *The Bride's Cookbook* by Poppy Cannon—a farewell gift from my mother who couldn't boil water either and was proud of it. The book was full of helpful household hints for the rookie homemaker, as well as easy, inventive recipes, many of them shortcuts using convenience foods—new in the marketplace since the end of World War II—which Cannon would enhance with a dash of this and a dollop of that. (A popular food writer, she had been the food editor of *Ladies Home Journal* and *House Beautiful*, and had previously published *The Can Opener Cookbook*, in which every ingredient was either canned, frozen, or powdered. (She once claimed that she could create an entire Thanksgiving dinner from convenience foods.) Under Poppy Cannon's expert guidance, I slowly and painstakingly taught myself to cook and keep house.

I really didn't have any expectations about my marriage and motherhood; I was just putting one foot in front of the other, trying each day to adjust to my new and completely unfamiliar circumstances in San Antonio at Lackland Air Force Base. At first I was terribly lonely and homesick. But Red had been brought up in a "Norman Rockwell family" without servants and governesses; he was used to pitching in and helping out—and that was a big help to me. My mother must have been worried about me, although she never actually said so. Instead, packages arrived on my doorstep—a cozy, woolen bathrobe, some flannel nightgowns, a box of stylish mix-and-match maternity skirts and blouses—all of which I loved and started wearing right away.

After four weeks of indoctrination at Lackland, where we lived on the base in a furnished apartment, Red received his orders for six months of primary flight training in Hondo, a dusty hamlet fifty miles due west of San Antonio. The highway to Hondo was as straight as a ribbon, and there was no speed limit in that part of west Texas. On the outskirts of the town, a small sign proclaimed: HONDO, TEXAS. POPULATION: 400.

We moved into an unfurnished, prefabricated, two-bedroom bungalow on the base, surrounded by a sea of other bungalows exactly the same as ours, and started making friends. My parents had given us a wedding check before we left New Jersey to cover extraneous expenses, and a discount furniture store in San Antonio enabled us to transform our little shack into a home of our own. I was apprehensive about my ongoing pregnancy and upcoming delivery—the baby was due in mid-February. We had heard horror stories about the maternity care at Lackland (there was no hospital, only an infirmary on the Hondo base), and shared them with our respective parents. A Princeton classmate of my father's, who lived in San Antonio, recommended a local obstetrician. Halfway through my pregnancy, I was relieved of some of my anxieties under his reassuring manner and professional care. He was strict about my diet and weight (I gained only fifteen pounds during the pregnancy), and assured me that I would be pain- free during the delivery, since I would be receiving a general anesthetic.

My mother and father wanted to be on hand for the birth; on my monthly drives into San Antonio (at eighty or ninety miles an hour) to see my doctor, I scouted out hotels and found one that I knew would please them. At dinner there, the second night of their stay, I went into labor. Instead of returning together to Hondo, Red deposited me at Nix Memorial Hospital in San Antonio. I was taken in hand by several competent nurses, and after that, everything became a blur until I woke up in a sunny hospital room the following morning. My mother was sitting quietly in a chair in the corner of the room, reading her latest selection from the Book-of-the-Month Club. She looked up and saw that I was awake.

"Joan," she asked me with a lilt in her voice, "do you know that you're the mother of a son?"

In the early morning hours of Valentine's Day, 1955, my first son, Ricky (Derrik Jr.), had been born, and I had no recollection of it.

*

Sex was not recommended during the last month of pregnancy and the first month after delivery. That was fine with me, since it still wasn't my favorite thing. My San Antonio doctor had fitted me with a diaphragm, but it was a nuisance and I was sloppy about using it. By early fall of 1955, I found myself pregnant again.

By this time—after six months in Hondo—we had moved for six months of advanced flight training to Lubbock, a college town in the panhandle of northwest Texas, the home of Texas Tech University. Lubbock was also known for the severe sandstorms that blew down from the north across the wide, flat plains of Oklahoma, closing everything down for a day or two, as hurricanes did back in the northeast. Along their path, the high winds would break off the tumbleweed bushes—peculiar ball-shaped, thorny plants, very dry and light—that thrived in the sandy soil of the region, and bounce them around for miles. These huge, weird spheres of tumbleweed would roll up against the doors and windows of our base housing. I finally understood the cowboy song, "Tumblin' Tumbleweed," that we had sung in music class over and over again at the Shrewsbury School.

Two thousand miles from home, I continued to throw myself into the role of wife, homemaker, and mother. By the time Red was transferred for his last year of compulsory service to Fort Knox, Kentucky, outside of Louisville, I was feeling useful and valuable and in control of my world. Ricky was a towheaded one-year-old by then; he had been a very alert, precocious baby, climbing out of his crib at six months and starting to walk on his own by holding on to the furniture. I loved reading to him and teaching him the alphabet. When James (nicknamed Jimmy) was born in April 1956, I flew back from Louisville to The Place, where my mother's staff could look after Ricky, then fourteen months old, while I spent the requisite five days of recovery at Monmouth Memorial Hospital. Jimmy became my "monkey," climbing up and falling off things—chairs, tables, stairs, bicycles, even trees—at an early age, on his way to later becoming a talented athlete.

Lisa was born in November 1957—a sweet, cuddly baby, completely bald at first, with her father's china-blue eyes and the sunniest disposition. We had settled down in the suburbs; Uncle Fred had died, leaving me enough money in his will for a down payment on a charming three-bedroom Cape Cod Colonial in Chatham, New Jersey. College friends who had married lived around the corner. Red was commuting to Wall Street, deeply involved in building his career, but he usually managed to get home in time to give Lisa her bottle and help out with the boys at bath time, while I made dinner. I was excited about my life and proud of my accomplishments; I had found my calling; I had secured my Norman Rockwell family at last.

The Place, only an hour away, continued to figure importantly in our lives. We celebrated every Thanksgiving and Christmas and many birthdays there, and spent several weeks there in the summers. Eventually, the children learned to swim in the same saltwater pool at the Ocean Beach Club where Tommy and I had learned to dive and swim, and where my father had exercised with his physical therapist after his devastating accident in 1945. They, too, started falling under the spell of The Place.

In 1959, three months after our fourth child Thomas (nicknamed Teke) was born, we bundled everyone into the station wagon and drove to The Place for Christmas. Red's parents were also joining us for the holiday, as they had since our marriage five years earlier. Soon after we arrived, I was upstairs changing Teke's diaper on the "big guest room" bed, when Margaret, who now lived with her husband in a neighboring town and was helping in the kitchen, came in to take a look at the new baby. Teke was long and skinny with big fingers and toes. Margaret studied him carefully.

"Well," she commented, "he's not the most beautiful baby in the world. But look how his little mouth turns up at the corners! He's got a sense of humor!"

Teke grew to be six feet four inches, the tallest of the three boys. His droll sense of humor and joie de vivre would charm the world.

But Christmas that year was not the merriest for me. Since Teke's birth I had been going through an unexpected sea change. Slowly, I was beginning to realize that despite my nun-like dedication to *kinder* and *küchen*, the college romance had not—for me—evolved into a mature marital relationship. Red was now completely focused on his career, and had started traveling for the firm. While he was away, I had time at home to reflect; I was more relaxed and content during his absences. When he returned and we were together in the household, I was painfully aware that we didn't share the same thoughts and feelings about things. When I tried to talk to him, we were miles apart. No matter how serious or superficial the subject was—where to send Ricky to Sunday School, or what to serve friends at our next dinner party—we were never on the same page. Red would have a flip, breezy answer, and that was that. I had gone out and done what Alistair Cooke had told me and my Smith classmates to do on that halcyon June day in 1954—but I had built my house on a flimsy foundation.

My parents, as usual, were oblivious to my unhappiness, but my mother-in-law, with whom I had become friends, somehow sensed it. At noon on Christmas Day, we were sitting alone on the big sofa in the living room, waiting for everyone to gather for the mid-day festivities, when she asked me what was wrong. I tried, gently, to share my misery.

"I just can't talk to him anymore," I started to explain, my eyes filling up with tears.

"You have so much on your plate, Joan, and you're doing such a great job," she said, trying to soothe my anguish. "Besides, relationships change over the years," she added, referring perhaps to her own marital difficulties, which I was aware of but which she rarely talked about.

I knew she didn't want to hear any more. What I didn't know was that it would be the last Christmas we would all be together on The Place.

*

As the new year of 1960 unfolded, my unhappiness intensified. I tried to share my feelings with Red, but, as in the past, I couldn't get his ear. Once again, I knew I would have to turn to my mother—since she and my father had engineered the marriage.

I asked her to come for lunch—which she did frequently—and while the four children were napping, I tried to describe how my feelings for Red had eroded, and how misunderstood and alienated I felt. After a brief silence, she responded.

"Are you still physically attracted to Red?" was her opening question.

I was dumbfounded. What did sex have to do with anything? Didn't she understand how profoundly miserable I was?

"I hate sex!" I lashed out. I wanted to hurt her, shock her, punish her for her stupidity and lack of compassion. "It's done nothing but get me in trouble!"

*

That spring, my parents sent us to a brilliant New York City psychiatrist (whom they had met at a dinner party at the apartment of friends on Park Avenue), hoping to salvage the marriage. Red and I met with him together initially; individual consultations followed. He also met with my parents and talked by phone with my in-laws.

Finally, I had someone in my life who listened and empathized with my misery. He strongly advised a trial separation for three months over the summer, allowing Red and me a cooling off period and time to think things through. (Years later, my parents told me that he had confided in them at the time that I was "on the verge of a nervous breakdown" and that he would not be responsible for my mental stability if we continued living together.) Red moved into Manhattan, nearer his workplace, hoping that I would come to my senses and eventually take him back. But I knew I had married the wrong man, and at the end of the three months, after several more psychiatric consultations, I asked Red for a divorce.

My father was distressed; he sank into a deep depression, claiming that our family's impeccable reputation was now blackened by its first divorce. My mother was angry and upset; once again, I had toppled her perfect world. My in-laws were also furious and stopped talking to me. But a year later, sanctioned by the brilliant psychiatrist, my wishes were granted, my divorce finalized on the grounds of incompatibility.

After six years of marriage and a year of separation, I was starting over again. It was 1961; I was a divorcée with four children, living in suburbia where the term "single parent" had yet to be invented. I had lost my Norman Rockwell family, but I still wanted to be the loving, attentive mother that my own mother hadn't been. I renewed my devotion to my adorable daughter, Lisa, and my three lovable sons; Ricky, the oldest, was about to enter kindergarten in Short Hills—we had moved there from Chatham for its excellent public school system. My parents, finally resigned to the situation, agreed to help support me. And The Place was our haven, our home-away-from-home, where we were always welcome. It continued to dominate our lives.

*

For some reason, my mother insisted that I hire a live-in housekeeper to help with running the household and raising the children. Maybe she wanted me to have the freedom to come and go, in the hopes of finding a second husband; maybe she felt I was incapable of managing everything alone. Her motives were never made clear to me, and I complied with her wishes. After interviewing a few candidates, I hired Hilda Brooks, a stocky, middle-aged brunette with a thick brogue, who turned out to be a jack-of-all-trades. Not only was she an excellent cook and adept at rudimentary carpentry, she also made delicious shortbread and extraordinary birthday cakes (she had worked in a bakery in Glasgow). If I gave a pirate-themed birthday party for one of the boys, she would create a treasure chest out of sheet cake; there were also fire engines, locomotives and fairy tale castles. She could even hang wallpaper.

Hilda had actually lost a thumb while working in a defense plant in Scotland during World War II, but chose to tell the children that the same fate would befall them if they sucked their thumbs. She was also an inveterate smoker, a two-inch ash frequently dangling precariously from the end of her cigarette as she moved around the house. (Teke, who was too young to dress himself, remembers being terrified that the ash would fall into his eye. He also remembers Hilda chasing and screaming at Jim, who was too fast for her.)

Hilda created boundaries, gave orders, handed out chores. Lisa probably got the best of her, accompanying her on several summer trips back to Glasgow to visit family.

I think all four children must have been a bit afraid of her. They certainly remember her as strict and unloving. But it turns out they were not angry and resentful—as I had been at my mother over the seemingly everlasting presence of Mamzelle. (I distinctly remember coming home from dates when I was a teenager and undressing for bed in the dim light of my walk-in closet so as not to wake Mamzelle—who still shared my bedroom. She finally left us to work for another family when Tommy, at age fourteen, went off to The Lawrenceville School). Hilda was with us for only a few years; after that I relied on day help.

Nevertheless, looking back later, I recognized that, for those few years at least, I had unwittingly adopted my mother's ways—allowing an unloving outsider to take over as the disciplinarian of my four children.

*

In the fall of 1961, Tommy phoned from the city and asked if he could come out for dinner. I was surprised to hear from him. He always included me (and Red and myself during our marriage) at bachelor parties he gave at his apartment and in the mansion; I also saw him at The Place on birthday celebrations and holidays. But he rarely called and never came out to the suburbs to visit me and the children.

Tommy was very intelligent and insightful—his Lawrenceville classmates had nicknamed his "the Judge." He dreamed about becoming a doctor. But he had always been an uneven student (probably due to undiagnosed dyslexia, which in those days was not a household word—students who combined high I.Q.s with erratic academic records were known as "underachievers"). He graduated from Lawrenceville but flunked out of Brown senior year with only one semester to go. At my father's suggestion, he had gone to work at Cowen and Company, never completing his degree. He was one of the funniest people I had ever known, but I worried about his drinking.

In my living room, we poured scotch and added ice. He downed his drink quickly, then poured himself a second, stronger one. "I've got something to tell you," he said. "I've asked Connie to marry me."

I was thrilled to hear this news, happy that he was ready to settle down and give up his bachelorhood.

"But there's something else," he continued. "Connie is jealous of my relationship with you. I can't be involved in your life anymore."

I was completely taken aback. I didn't think of us as having a close, ongoing relationship. He had not been "involved in my life" since I left The Place—married and pregnant—seven years before in September of 1954, at the start of his sophomore year at Brown.

Clearly, my brother was abandoning me, or was it the other way around? Perhaps he felt that I had abandoned him when I left The Place so suddenly. My unexpected departure must have been a shock and a disappointment to him; he probably had envisioned much more from me—a full-blown career in journalism, perhaps. I also suspected that Red had not been his ideal choice as a brother-in-law. But we had never discussed these things.

I wondered if he had me up on a pedestal, admired me, idolized me—the pretty, older sister who sailed through school, always getting good grades, while he had struggled academically. Maybe Connie interpreted this admiration as some kind of "crush" that engendered her jealousy. Or maybe she hadn't actually asked him to become uninvolved; maybe for his own personal reasons he had to disenthrall himself from me.

He and Connie had been dating in the city for several years. Everyone, including myself, liked her tremendously and thought she was a stabilizing influence on my brother. I didn't comment on his "something else"; it didn't occur to me to defend my rights as his only sister and sibling, to demand that he sustain a relationship with me as well as with Connie. I responded passively and just nodded my head.

"I think it's great that you and Connie are getting married, Tom. Everybody loves Connie," I told him, and let it go at that.

CHAPTER TWELVE

Across a Crowded Room

———

T he living room at The Place was filled with familiar people smoking, drinking, chatting—my brother's friends from Brown and various wives and dates—on a Saturday evening in mid-November 1963. I had driven to the mansion alone for Tommy's Brown-Princeton cocktail party, which was held every other year after the football game in Palmer Stadium on the Princeton campus—only an hour from the estate.

Across the crowded room, I noticed my parents talking to a rugged young man I had never seen before. My attraction to him was intense and immediate. I felt a magnetic pull, and wove my way through the guests to be introduced.

Mike Bowman was a legendary Princeton football captain; I had heard about him over the years but we had never crossed paths. He had come to the party with a Brown classmate of my brother's; at the time they were working together in the business department of *The New Yorker*. They were single, lived in Manhattan and both had dates in tow that evening. Mike and I freshened our drinks, and soon the two of us were huddled in a corner, conversing intently as if we had known each other for years. Most of our conversation revolved around his mentor, the revered Princeton football coach Charlie Caldwell, and his controversial second wife Lucy, both of whom had been close friends of my parents before Caldwell's untimely death from colon cancer not long after Mike's graduation in 1957. But the chemistry between us—at least for me—was palpable.

I could have gone on listening and talking for hours, but we were eventually interrupted and swallowed up in the crowd. An hour later, when I saw him leaving with his date, I rushed over to the front door. I said goodbye and shook his hand. "I really loved talking to you, Mike," I told him. I wanted him to remember me, although I didn't expect to hear from him ever again.

Six days later, on November 22, I sat in my car, waiting for Ricky to finish an after-school Cub Scout meeting. I casually flipped on the radio and heard the heart-stopping news from Dallas: in a horrific act of violence, President John F. Kennedy had been assassinated. I burst out crying and for a moment lost my breath.

While on a two-day tour in Texas, accompanied by Vice-President Lyndon Johnson and their respective wives, the President had been shot in the left shoulder and the head in his motorcade, with Jackie unharmed at his side; he had died an hour later at Parkland Hospital from severe brain trauma. In a split second, the idea of this country as a peace-loving nation, full of reverence and respect for our leaders—a concept that I and many others had fervently believed in—was shattered forever. (Five years later, in 1968, when Martin Luther King, Jr., age thirty-nine, and Robert Kennedy, age forty-three, were assassinated within two months of each other, we would be reminded that there were madmen in our society—lone, alienated killers with access to guns—executing despicable acts of violence. Once again we would feel shocked and betrayed by these unexpected, evil events).

Kennedy had been the second youngest President (after Theodore Roosevelt); the first President born in the twentieth century; the youngest President elected to office (at age forty-three); the first and only Catholic President; the only President to have won a Pulitzer Prize (for *Profiles in Courage*, published in 1955). Whether or not you agreed with his politics, his youth and vigor had inspired hope both here and all over the world. Elected in 1960, he and his stunning wife Jackie, then thirty-one, had brought glamour and excitement not only to the White House but everywhere they traveled around the globe.

The news was paralyzing; across the nation, everything came to a standstill. Schools, businesses, government offices were shut down; sporting events and performances were canceled. For the first time in the history of television in this country, all scheduled programs and commercials were canceled during the ensuing days of national mourning; only footage related to the assassination and the funeral were shown.

Certain iconic images became sealed in my memory from those dreadful days: Jackie, splattered with her husband's blood—in her pink wool, Chanel-style suit and matching pillbox hat—trying to crawl out of the back seat on to the trunk of the limousine, to avoid the line of fire, seconds after he has been shot; Vice-President Lyndon Johnson, ninety-nine minutes after Kennedy's death, being sworn in as the next President on Air Force One, flanked by his wife Lady Bird and Jackie, still wearing her bloodstained pink suit; two days later, on November 24, Lee Harvey Oswald, Kennedy's accused assassin, being fatally shot in the stomach by Jack Ruby—an unsavory nightclub owner with possible links to organized crime—in the basement of the Dallas police headquarters; four days later on November 25, his third birthday, John-John standing with his sister Caroline, age six, and his mother Jackie veiled in black, saluting his father's flag-draped casket as it was carried past them outside of St. Matthew's Cathedral in Washington after the Requiem Mass.

The assassination was cataclysmic. This country's history was forever scarred; none of us would ever be the same. But slowly, life resumed its normal pace; daily routines started up again. And much to my surprise, I received a phone call from Mike Bowman. We started dating, and it wasn't long before I was not only hooked but also hoping for a marriage proposal. I was in love, I was loved, and I was having fun for the first time in years.

Mike was a thirty-year-old carefree bachelor when I met him in the living room at The Place; I was a thirty-two-year old divorcée with four children. He was gifted, charismatic, popular—a big bear of a man, full of tall stories and *bon mots*—with a huge circle of friends and acquaintances. He referred to our relationship, with a laugh, as a "sociological nightmare." "Opposites attract because they have so much in common," he would say to me, with a twinkle in his eyes. And there was no question that we were powerfully attracted to one another, on every level.

Mike was of Anglo-Irish heritage, and was raised in a broken, impoverished family in the outskirts of Boston. His father had abandoned him and his mother when he was two years old; his mother, despite her Roman-Catholic upbringing, had remarried several times, bringing Mike a half-brother and half-sister, each ten years apart. During his four years at a Catholic high school in Newton, Mike moved in with his maternal grandmother—the rock of the family—and became a famous schoolboy athlete, excelling in basketball and football. His mother wanted him to become a policeman, but his high school coaches had more ambitious goals for him. He worked his way through Princeton on scholarship—the first member of his blue-collar family to attend college. He had been captain of every football team he had ever played on.

Mike also had a dark, moody side, but I was used to that with my father, and chose to overlook his unstable behavior. He fascinated me. I remember his description of his earliest childhood memory. "I was very small, and I was sitting in the middle of a dirt road outside of a house—I have no idea how I got there—and suddenly I was run over by a car. I wasn't hurt, but it was terrifying."

Apocryphal or not, this bleak recollection, not only frightening but also fraught with neglect and abandonment, was in sharp contrast to my magical memory of skating with my father. Perhaps if I had paid closer attention, I would have been more insightful about Mike's inner darkness and had second thoughts about marriage. But I still harbored inner feelings of inadequacy and not belonging—carried over from my childhood—and Mike's legendary accomplishments and charismatic personality covered up and compensated for those demons. I became completely addicted to him, and I believed he adored me. I thought of him as the love of my life; I thought we had everything. I was also in rescuer mode, believing I could give him everything he had never had—a faithful wife, a stable home, a loving family. By the time we were married four years later, Mike had embarked on a meteorically successful career on Wall Street. By February 1972, our first son, Michael Jr. (nicknamed Bo), was three years old, and our second son, Jonathan (nicknamed Jon), was born on Leap Year Day.

Under the influence of his grandmother, a devout Roman Catholic and daily communicant, Mike had been brought up in the Church. When he asked me to marry, he also asked me to convert to his faith. It seemed important to him, although he did not attend Mass during the years of our courtship. I hoped that sharing our faith would bring us even closer together. We spoke to the priests at my local parish, where I started six months of instructions, ending with my being received into the Church by baptism a few weeks before our marriage in September of 1967.

We chose the United Nations Chapel for our wedding ceremony—a small, dramatically contemporary space on a side street near U.N. Headquarters where Pope Paul VI—the first Pope in history to visit New York City—had celebrated Mass in 1965. Two priests were in residence there—one Irish-American and one African-American. I was very impressed with the latter—a very tall, imposing figure with a mellifluous voice who was appointed the Bishop of Harlem a few years later. When I told Mike that I wanted him to marry us, his reaction was immediate and unequivocal.

"Are you kidding, Joan? We'll have the rich Park Avenue Jews on your side of the church, the poor Boston Irish Catholics on my side, and the Smith and Princeton WASPS sprinkled all over the place.

And you want to throw a black priest into the mix? No way!"

Once again I responded passively, reluctant to fight back. And that was the end of that. Nevertheless, the wedding was a euphoric occasion for me, with a reception following the ceremony at the elegant Georgian Suite on East 77ⁿᵈ Street (engineered by my mother, who was thrilled to be giving a "real" wedding at last for her only daughter). One hundred and twenty relatives and friends attended; the four children were on hand throughout, looking adorable in their Sunday best. My fervent hopes for a happy, fulfilling marriage to the man of my dreams were now under way. I believed I had chosen a loving husband, an attentive stepfather and a proud father-to-be for our future children.

I was also passionate about my newfound religion, coming in from years of spiritual limbo to the "one true apostolic faith." I loved reading the Gospels and the stories of all the saints; I loved the sense of community that surrounded me at weekly Mass; I found the repetitive rituals of the Mass soothing and secure. But I'm not sure I could have felt so passionately about the Roman Catholic faith had it not been for the example and influence of Angelo Roncalli.

After the death of Pope Pius XII in 1958, Roncalli had been elected, at the age of seventy-seven, as a compromise candidate on the twelfth ballot, taking the name of Pope John XXIII. The third of thirteen children born into a peasant family, he had risen to become a cardinal and the patriarch of Venice in 1953. During World War II, as the papal delegate in Turkey, he had devoted himself to the care of refugees, especially Jews. He obtained transit visas to Palestine for some; to others he issued baptismal certificates that would enable them to pass as Christians, with the understanding that no baptisms need be performed. Through Roncalli, thousands of Jews were rescued.

Roncalli was a Modernist; as Pope, his concerns were for the whole world and all humankind, not solely for the Church. He broke the tradition of the Pope as a prisoner of the Vatican by traveling outside Rome. His homely figure, directness and warmth made a huge impact around the world—both on TV and in person—even on non-Catholics. He was described as "the only man ... in whose company one feels the physical sensation of peace." He convened the Second Vatican Council (the First Council had met in 1869) to work on the *aggiornamento*—the updating—of the Church; by the time of his death in 1963 (the year I met Mike) he had instigated sweeping changes.

Under his influence, the Council voted for the Mass to be said in the vernacular; had it still been said in Latin I don't think I would have found it so accessible and heartwarming. Because of his reforms we were allowed to attend Mass on Saturdays instead of Sundays, and face-to-face confessions were permitted and encouraged, replacing the anonymous secrecy of the confessional box. There was even a "Folk Mass" every weekend with guitars replacing the organ, and familiar gospel songs instead of hymns, which Bo and Jonathan loved attending with me. Occasionally Mike would also join us, but my wish that our shared faith would bring us closer together was not fulfilled; Mike's attendance at Mass was sporadic and unpredictable.

His behavior at home was also unpredictable. The moodiness that I had been aware of during our courtship still prevailed at times; at other times he was bursting with charm and energy, almost manic. He was extremely focused on building his career on Wall Street, which included entertaining clients after work well into the evening hours; there were nights when he didn't return or even call to let me know his whereabouts. I believed him when he consoled me back at home, telling me how much he loved me and that we shared something special. In the meantime, his successes as an institutional salesman and trader were becoming legendary, camouflaging his dark side.

*

I was almost forty years old when Jonathan was born on Leap Year Day, 1972, well aware that my childbearing years were over. I can't explain what triggered it, but gradually, during Jonathan's first year—with my family now complete—I experienced another unexpected sea change. For the first time in my life I wanted to do something that was all and only mine—away from the nurturing role of wife and mother that had consumed me since my college graduation. Mike was sympathetic and encouraged me to seek out career counseling. I had heard about the services offered at Stevens Institute of Technology in Hoboken, only half an hour from our home, and I made an appointment for a day and a half of testing, with the promise of results and recommendations by the end of the second day.

Early on the morning of my first appointment, my housekeeper, who came in to help out on weekdays, called in sick. My disappointment was intense when I realized I would have to reschedule at Stevens, but Mike offered to stay home from the office until I got back from my first round of testing. He seemed to sense how important this was to me—more important than even I realized at the time.

Before embarking on six hours of written personality and aptitude tests, my counselor—a kindly middle-aged man with a sympathetic ear—interviewed me. "What are you really good at?" he asked.

I was stunned, embarrassed and speechless. I had spent the first major part of my life in school, the second running a household and raising six children. The painful truth was—I wasn't good at anything.

But I had to cough something up. "I give great dinner parties," I told him sheepishly.

"Really!" he exclaimed. "How interesting. Tell me—what part do you like best? Preparing for them, or actually giving them?"

"Oh, I love everything!" I answered enthusiastically. "I love planning the menu and doing the cooking and setting the table and getting the house ready—and I really love bringing all the people together."

It was a beginning.

The testing revealed that it was important for me to have variety in my day-to-day work, and that I liked to influence people. My scores were off the chart in journalism and interior design, with high scores also as a teacher, performer and—much to my amusement—a mortician. I chose to ignore the latter three career paths, but I had secretly dreamed of being a designer ever since I was a teenager, although I had never shared my fantasy with anyone. Perhaps it was a result of the discrepancy between my lonely, isolated childhood and the magical surroundings I grew up in, but the combination of people and houses had always fascinated me.

Mike and I laughed together at the thought of my becoming a mortician. Years later, reflecting back, I would recognize a subtle connection between the skills of a mortician and the skills of an interior designer. My desire to create beautiful environments, to make homes out of houses, to draw warmth from combining inanimate objects, to use color to brighten the lives of people and soft fabrics to comfort them—all contributed to a way of soothing people's every day lives, not unlike the comfort and soothing that a mortician extends to those in mourning, but without the tragic overtones.

At The Baldwin School and Smith College, I had learned to organize, to think independently, and to work to the best of my abilities. These tools gave me the confidence to set out on my own and pursue a career in residential design. Over the summer months of 1974, a series of intensive courses at the New York School of Interior Design allowed me get started. Over the years, I had forgotten how much I had enjoyed school during my student days. The design courses were stimulating and challenging, and one special teacher became my mentor and introduced me to the more sophisticated nuances of the work. A chance meeting with an acquaintance who needed to refurbish her elegant home nearby presented me with my first client, while I continued my studies. She and her husband referred me to friends, and by 1975 I was off and running.

Every job was an adventure for me. I had been trained by my mentor to be flexible, to be a good listener, and to think of myself as an interpreter. I discovered I had a gift not only for working with color and space but, more importantly, for incorporating my clients' personalities and possessions into pleasing, comfortable rooms. My work brought joy and excitement into their lives, and taught them to appreciate the visual world around them in new and different ways. And I loved running my own business.

My mother, intrigued with my new career, asked me to help her with ongoing renovations in the mansion. We spruced up the dining and living rooms, and redecorated a few of the guest rooms. We had fun together, and I think she was proud of my talents and skills. But my father never mentioned my work to me. Perhaps he thought of it as only a hobby that I was infatuated with. Now in his eighties, there were many days when he didn't feel well. He became quiet and more introspective, and was prone to reminiscing about all the changes that had occurred since his birth in 1893. "I've gone from the horse and carriage to the jet engine," he said to me incredulously, during one of my visits to The Place. But he never shared any other feelings with me as he reflected back on his life.

My counselor at Stevens had understood clearly that my complex family at the time— four teenagers from my first marriage and two young children from my second—would not provide the necessary tranquility for writing. But during our final session he tried to extract a commitment from me. "Your scores in journalism and your editorial skills are so high," he told me. "Promise me that eventually you'll pursue the writing. At the very least, you can write about design."

I nodded compliantly, knowing I could never possibly accomplish anything of the sort, and put it out of my mind.

CHAPTER THIRTEEN

My Mother, Myself

———

Once again, I'm sitting with my mother on the big, comfortable sofa in the living room, overlooking the expansive front lawn of the mansion with its towering old trees— where I skated with my father forty-five years before. Earlier today, January 15, 1981, he died of congestive heart failure—at age eighty-eight—in the master bedroom upstairs.

His death this morning did not come as a sudden surprise; he hadn't been well for a few years, and was bedridden with round-the-clock nurses for several weeks. I've been prepared for his death for some time, and am strangely unmoved by his passing. But even though my father had been slowly deteriorating and was terminally ill for over a month, I know my mother is devastated. I've driven to The Place, an hour away from my home in northern New Jersey, to spend the afternoon with her. Tommy, on a business trip in Cleveland, will not arrive until tomorrow, when the three of us will plan the memorial service.

My mother's oldest friend Lize has stopped by to extend her condolences. Lize had married during her middle years, has no children and is now a widow, still living a few miles away on Pullman Avenue in Elberon. She sits near us in my father's favorite red leather chair, listening attentively while my mother reminisces about their wonderful years together, how much they had shared, how compatible they had always been, how they had always loved the same things, especially their life on the estate. "It was more important to us than anything," she acknowledges. "We had an understanding ... an agreement ... if we ever had to give up things, we would try and hold on to this. We just loved everything here."

She sits quietly for a moment, lost in thought, then suddenly looks up at her old friend, ignoring my presence. "You know, Lize, I wouldn't care if I died in my sleep tonight. Now that Eddie's gone, my life is over. I've got nothing left to live for."

My mother is seventy-eight years old; I'm forty-eight. I'm sitting right next to her—her only daughter, mother of six of her eight grandchildren. Over the years, I think I have learned exactly what to expect from her. My harsh hatreds have been blunted, my painful resentments have evolved into a dull ache of acceptance. I believe I understand her limitations. But today her words, sudden and unexpected, make me feel totally worthless and forlorn—the way I had felt so often as a child. The sting is still there. And worst of all, she's completely unaware of it.

Silence invades the sunny living room. I stare down at my lap, embarrassed and speechless, wondering if Lize—who has never had a daughter—can possibly imagine how hurtful and humiliating these words are to me.

Then my mother sighs and straightens up a bit. "Well, at least now I'll have a chance to get to know my grandchildren. And it's about time I learned how to cook."

I think of these pronouncements—her desire either to die that night, or to get to know her grandchildren, or to learn to cook—as her three wishes. But a few months later, settling into widowhood, she seems to have forgotten them. Instead, encouraged by the daughter of an old friend, she begins doing volunteer work nearby at CPC Mental Health Services, teaching the mentally retarded to knit and crochet and embroider, crafts at which she had always excelled. She shows an amazing aptitude for dealing with them. They can't wait for her sessions, gathering around her like ardent children, captivated by the sweetness of her patience and enthusiasm. She wins the volunteer-of-the-year award several times, but never shares any thoughts or feelings about her work with me. I can't avoid the painful thought that she can now give to the disabled what she was never able to give to me.

As a widow, she also pursues an active social life, driving herself to New York City where she stays at the Carlyle or the Stanhope, lunching and dining with summer friends, keeping up with the latest Broadway openings and Hollywood movies. She drives to Connecticut to spend weekends with Tommy and his family. She and I meet often for lunch at a charming French bistro located halfway between our New Jersey homes, where we chat about inconsequential things—a new hair salon she has visited, or a recent servant crisis in the household. But she seems vulnerable and needy without Eddie there to protect her; she has become dependent on me and Tommy for the first time in her life.

*

A few weeks after the death of my father, my mother called me at home, inviting me to spend seven days with her on Longboat Key in Sarasota, Florida—the first week of a three-week getaway from the cold northeastern weather that she is planning. I accept gratefully, looking forward to an escape not only from the bleak weather but also from the everyday stress at home—Bo and Jonathan's challenges at school, the details of my design business, Mike's ongoing problems with drugs, alcohol and depression.

Now, two years have passed; I'm relishing my third visit to this small, charming Florida hotel on the Gulf of Mexico. I spend my days here indulging in a hedonistic routine. In the mornings, after breakfast with my mother in her room, I walk on the beach, followed by a swim and a sunbath. After lunch together on the hotel patio, we drive to a local museum or to the nearby town on a shopping expedition. Before meeting for cocktails and dinner, where friends of hers also vacationing in the Sarasota area often join us, I have time in the afternoons to catch up on my reading—old *New Yorker* magazines or a recently published novel by a favorite author.

The days take on a calm, reassuring rhythm, in sharp contrast to my hectic daily schedule back in New Jersey.

This is my last morning before returning home. Lying here on my beach chair, drenched by the tropical sun after my morning swim, the salt water dries on my body in tiny, shiny beads. I feel like a sun-baked shell, washed clean by the warm, soothing surf. I am completely relaxed. But the staccato hammering of a downy wood-pecker in a nearby banyan tree reminds me that in a few hours I will be leaving this peaceful place. I haven't told my mother that I'm worried about what I'm returning to. Although I have not heard a stinging remark from her since the day my father died, I know she still doesn't want to hear about unpleasantness. She certain-ly doesn't want me to confide that, after fifteen years of marriage, Mike's problems—which over the years she has shown no interest in—are escalating, and that my marriage is in serious jeopardy.

The gentle sighing of the tide beckons me for one last dip. Then I throw on a floral cover-up and my red sandals and make my way to the hotel patio for our final lunch here together. I have never shared my conflicted feelings about her to any friends or family members; to the outside world we are a typically loving mother and daughter. And ironically, as she has aged, her facial features have softened and mine have become more angular; I've started resembling her more than my father.

Sitting congenially at our table under the green and white striped umbrella—next to the pansy bed, with the sea-grape trees screen-ing the sun behind us—I can almost believe that my pain of years past is just a figment of my imagination. As we sip our drinks and order our salads in the cooling breeze, I hear the bartenders and waiters and some of the guests at adjoining tables saying to each other, "Isn't it wonderful how much they look alike? Isn't it mar-velous how well they get along?" And the sea-grape leaves rustle behind us, and the pansies nod their inky faces in approval.

*

When my mother drops me off at the airport a few hours later, I jump out of the car and grab my suitcase off the back seat. Then, still under the spell of our tropical lifestyle, and not quite ready to face the painful realities of my everyday world back in New Jersey, I lean back in through the open window on the passenger side. "I wish I could stay longer," I tell her.

"You're such a comfort to me, Joan." Her response takes me by surprise. She has never said anything this intimate to me before, nor will she ever again. Maybe somewhere in her heart she really loves me and is proud of me, I think to myself as I head into the airport. Then I realize that—after fifty years together—I'm still desperate for any sliver of affection from her.

CHAPTER FOURTEEN
Burying My Mother

I n her mid-eighties, a broken hip followed by a series of small strokes forced my mother to give up her volunteer teaching and her traveling about. She stayed on in her beloved house and retreated into a sedentary life. "I just don't feel well," she would tell me during our frequent phone calls.

Outside her windows, the aging property fell into disrepair. The gardens were permanently plowed under; the garage was partially destroyed by fire; the greenhouse burned to the ground. Layers of white paint peeled in large curls away from the clapboard of the old mansion, shutters hung askew, porches sagged. Inside the house, ceilings cracked, plaster blistered and faucets dripped. My mother was a wealthy widow, still surrounded by staff in the servants' wing, fully able to afford any renovations in the mansion or across the property. But she never seemed to care about or even notice the decay around her. Perhaps it comforted her to see the house somehow mirroring her own disintegration, for after all, she was only four years older than The Place.

Her last years were difficult, with frequent stays in the local hospital and round-the-clock nurses at home, as her health continued to fail. But she made up her mind to have us all for Christmas in 1989. I was fifty-seven years old, and had spent every Christmas of my life there. It was always her most favorite holiday; she must have sensed—as we all did—that it would be her last. Her hairdresser and manicurist had been to the house earlier in the week; when she came downstairs Christmas Eve to have supper and to open gifts with all of us, she looked elegant in a beautiful emerald green bathrobe that I had never seen before. But she appeared frail and weak and went to bed early. Christmas Day she joined us for midday dinner, but spent the rest of the afternoon and evening in her bedroom resting. Less than two months later, in the early morning hours of February 20, 1990, she died of congestive heart failure in the same bedroom she had shared with her sister Virginia growing up in the mansion, and with my father throughout their fifty-year marriage—the room she had slept in since the house was built in 1906. Next to her at her death was the vacant twin bed where my father had died nine years earlier.

I thought back to my mother's desires that day at The Place in 1981 when I sat with her and Lize in the living room planning my father's memorial service—either to die that night or to get to know her grandchildren or to learn how to cook—what I called her three wishes. None of them had ever come true.

According to her will, my mother was cremated, but she left no other instructions. Neither Tommy nor I had any interest in maintaining the estate; we had each established our own way of life with our families years ago—he in Connecticut, I in northern New Jersey. Even the beaches didn't beckon us any longer. Tommy and his family vacationed on Nantucket; my children and I had discovered Martha's Vineyard some years earlier—an island we all loved beyond reason—and I was spending every July there. We decided to give a simple memorial service in the house before we started the process of putting it up for sale and emptying it out, agreeing to bury her ashes later on in the spring in the family plot at a nearby cemetery in West Long Branch.

My mother had been a self-proclaimed atheist all her life, but Tommy felt strongly that we needed a religious touch. Lize suggested the rabbi from the Reform temple in Elberon; a tall, imposing man with a deep, sonorous voice, he agreed (although he had never met my mother) to open and close the brief service with a prayer. Tommy offered to give the eulogy; we also asked her doctor, who conveniently lived across the street, to speak (Doug Ackerman had retired). Nick had been particularly attentive to her in her final year, checking in on her every day, and she was inordinately fond of him.

"Wouldn't you like to say a few words?" my brother asked me on the phone from his home in Connecticut.

Tommy and I were still not close; we had never shared our respective feelings about our parents. I thought back again to the day my father died in the mansion in 1981, and my mother's stinging words about having nothing more to live for. My brother knew nothing about my torturous relationship with her. Nor was he aware that I hadn't mourned after my father died; I hadn't even shed a tear at his memorial service. Now, nine years later, I was once again unmoved by the death of a parent; I did not grieve or weep over my mother's passing. Over the years, I had tried to think of Ruth and Eddie as friendly strangers; since they were never loving parents— or what I imagined were loving parents—I felt that they had died for me in many ways before their natural deaths. That was how I coped with our lack of intimacy and their superficial interest in me and my family; that was my survival technique.

Until my mother's death I had been comfortable with this self-imposed emotional detachment. But now I was beginning to be aware that my true feelings—of hurt and abandonment—seemingly under control, were repressed and convoluted, and might start seeping out. Besides, how could I eulogize my mother with the years of pain varnished over in my heart?

I was also shielding Mike's ongoing problems from my family and the outside world. Since losing a position in December 1987 he had not been employed, and his erratic behavior and depression had intensified. I was afraid that any extra pressure—like speaking in front of a crowd—would crack my veneer and cause me to break down.

"No thanks, Tom." I answered without hesitation. "I don't think I can handle it. I know you and Nick will do a great job."

On a cold, dreary Sunday afternoon in late February, 1990, five days after her death, friends and family—almost a hundred strong—gathered from near and far to pay their last respects. We had pushed the furniture to the side and had filled the living room with folding chairs. I sat in the front row next to Mike—facing the dining room where my grandfather's portrait still hung over the mantel—surrounded by my six children, now ages eighteen to thirty-five. Suddenly I realized that we were all there to say farewell, not only to my mother, but also to the mansion, the lawns, the trees, the gardens, the old stone gateposts, the crunch of the gravel driveway, the tinkle of silver and crystal, the reassuring kitchen smells of freshly-baked pies and succulent roasts, the heady fragrance of freshly-picked flowers ...

For everyone knew it would be the last time they would be invited to the house. We were celebrating the end of an era, the death—after almost a century—of life on The Place.

*

During the weeks following the service, condolence notes poured in to Tommy and me from friends and acquaintances of all ages. Lize wrote from Arizona where she was visiting her sister-in-law: "Ruth has always been something very special to me. I always admired her great courage and fortitude. Surely these attributes were a great help to her these last difficult years. Her devotion to both of you and your families was outstanding." A younger acquaintance wrote from Florida: "I just heard of your mother's passing. The last of the grandes dames! So outstanding and a true lady!" A married couple—childhood friends of ours—wrote: "Your mother had her own style. She always looked so bandbox neat, never a wrinkle or a hair out of place ... It was a pleasure to see her ... in those later years. She would remember our children's names, and ask about them. We shall miss her. It feels like the end of an era." A local woman who had helped in the kitchen over the holidays and had often filled in on the regular cook's day-off sent a mass card and wrote in the enclosed note: "I worked for your mother and father for many years ... they were two of the best people to work for."

The daughter of old friends and neighbors of my parents, now both deceased, wrote: "Every Christmas morning—I cannot count the years—before our own Christmas dinner, we came to [your parents] open house [with] their huge friendly Christmas tree and a large circle of growing children, grandchildren, nieces and nephews and their children and others . . . It was always a scene of promise and fecundity for the approaching new year. In time I brought my own children too, Alissa and Hanna and to this day Hanna remembers Mr. Cowen with great warmth because when she was a young teenager he took time out from the holiday party to talk to her seriously about colleges."

The daughter of other old friends, who had originally encouraged her to volunteer after my father's death, wrote: "Your mother was very special. I cannot let her death go by without telling you how much she meant to the children and chronically ill older women at CPC. Simply put, they loved her. Through her classes on needlework, they talked with her about their lives, their problems, and Ruth with her directness and patience was there to help them with her support, her love and her strength. She became their role model. She will be sorely missed."

A close friend, who summered in West End and had spent many years as a social worker in Manhattan, wrote from Wisconsin where she was spending the winter with her daughter and her family: "As you know, your mother and I have had a very special relationship [since becoming widows] . . . although our personalities were very different, we agreed on the basics, like love of family and integrity in facing up to life's vicissitudes . . . you and your families should all feel good. You gave Ruth so much support, joy and love. I am glad you shared [her last] Christmas at The Homestead. Although it was a tremendous effort for her to 'swing' it, every minute was worth it to her ... I feel lucky having had such a gallant, lovely lady as a friend."

I wondered if my own persona, like my mother's—and my father's—was as different to my family at home as it was to my friends in the outside world. Would my children get letters like these after I was gone, describing someone they never knew?

*

A month or so after the memorial service, on a raw, windy April morning, we gathered in the cemetery a few miles from The Place, in front of the graves of my mother's parents Clarence and Flora, her sister Virginia and her two husbands, Freddie and Aaron, and Virginia's oldest daughter, my first cousin Ginny (who had died a year earlier from complications of alcoholism and emphysema). We were there to bury my mother's ashes in the family plot. Not knowing the protocol, I consulted with the director of the local funeral home, a lovely woman who had helped arrange the memorial service at the house. "Since you've already had a memorial service, Joan, some flowers and just a short prayer or a poem—nothing elaborate—will suffice," she advised. I passed this on to Tommy, who offered to say a few words.

We were only a handful of people—my husband Mike and me, Tommy and his wife Connie, their daughter Jennifer and her fiancé. My brother took a sheaf of notes from his coat pocket and began reading. I stood behind the others next to Mike, staring at my grandparents' gray marble tombstones—the grandparents I never knew—imagining their ghosts hovering nearby. As Tommy droned on and on from the Old Testament, the New Testament, Walt Whitman, Emily Dickinson, Shakespeare, Melville's *Moby Dick* and more, something came over me that I had never encountered before—a violent upheaval that started in my toes and wrenched its way upwards throughout my entire body, an outburst of desperate, wracking sobs.

I made my way back to our car nearby and sat in the front passenger seat, still sobbing endlessly and uncontrollably. A few moments later, when my brother had finally finished, Mike joined me. He sat in the driver's seat, as still as stone, while the emotional tornado drained out of me. He never touched me; he never questioned me; he never even spoke. There was no comfort—neither during my outburst nor after I was depleted.

Suddenly his self-absorption and lack of compassion struck me as unforgivable and unforgettable—emblematic of all the cruelty and abuse that he had inflicted on me, and that I had put up with, as his years of self-destruction had taken their toll on him, on me, on the children, on the marriage. It seemed that he was closed off in a circle of solitude; he lived apart right in the midst of things. I sat up with a jolt, realizing that I was locked in a toxic, co-dependent relationship with my husband—still trying to rescue him from his demons, still in denial that his instabilities and addictions were actually destroying my spirit. And at that moment, in the front seat of the car, I knew in my heart that inevitably—in a year or two or possibly even three—whenever I could summon up the emotional strength to deal with it, whenever the time seemed right, whenever … I would have to end my second marriage.

As my tears dried up we left the cemetery and drove back to The Place; Tommy and his family followed in their own car. It was the last time we would all be there in the house together. Over sandwiches and Chardonnay we divided up my mother's jewelry and fur coats, discussing the sale of the house and the distribution of its contents. Nobody spoke to me about my outburst. Perhaps they hadn't noticed; perhaps they had expected it and took it for granted; perhaps they just didn't know what to say or didn't even care.

Later on, when I thought about my loss of control that day at graveside, I realized that my mother's death and the death of our life on The Place had liberated me—opening up a readiness to face certain previously hidden realities. I was beginning to recognize the end of something that had never really started; my onslaught of tears was for what could have been but would now never be. I was finally starting to grieve—not for what was over, but rather for what had never happened.

At last, with the death of my mother, the family matriarch, and the forthcoming sale of the estate, I could break the spell of The Place—and release the padlock of my second marriage. Slowly, I could come to consciousness about what had been missing from my childhood—and what was still missing from my life. Burying my mother would allow me to unbury the truth.

CHAPTER FIFTEEN
Trays and Tears

————

I called in Anna, Frank the gardener's cousin—who had assisted over the years with spring cleaning in the mansion—to help me prepare the house for sale. We started in the kitchen, laundry room and servant's dining room, then worked our way into the pantry and adjoining main dining room. Frank had died several years earlier; as we emptied drawers, cupboards and closets Anna chattered away, reminiscing about his years of service on The Place.

I was only half-listening as we moved around from room to room, when Anna suddenly stopped talking. Then she sighed and blurted out, "How sad it was that your father caused that terrible accident!"

I stared at her in shock as I listened to the details of what had really happened when Frank drove my father to the West End station on that freezing winter's day in February 1945. Worried about missing his train, my father had urged Frank to step on the gas and cross the tracks immediately after the last car of the southbound train had passed, without waiting to look both ways for other oncoming trains. Frank was unwilling to hesitate or disobey. I had always known—since that disastrous day when I was twelve years old—that my father had been hit by his own train, but for almost fifty years I had never known that the accident was his own fault.

Frank had shared this knowledge with his relatives, but my parents had apparently kept it a secret from their friends and family. I wondered if my father had even shared it with my mother. How guilty he must have felt! No wonder he never complained after he was crippled. Now I also understood why he had insisted that Frank stay on, living over the garage rent-free, after he was too old and infirm to work on the property, and why his widow Jenny was still living there alone, her children grown and married, when my mother died.

As Anna and I continued our work throughout the kitchen areas and into dining room, we started collecting an inordinate number of trays. There were beautifully embossed sterling silver trays, probably left over from my grandparents' time, breakfast trays, tea trays, cocktail trays, hand-painted tole trays, wooden trays, lucite trays, cheese trays, hors d'oeuvres trays, special trays for chilling shrimp and caviar—all in all I must have counted over twenty trays. As I watched them piling up on the countertops, they soon became symbols in my mind of my parents' everyday existence in the mansion. It was a way of life, probably instilled in my mother by her own parents—who also had lived in the house surrounded by servants, overflowing with comforts—that remained supremely important, apparently to both my mother and father, above all else.

These trays were the totems of their marriage, but I had no use for any of them. I had left that hedonistic lifestyle behind when I drove away from The Place as a young, pregnant woman with my first husband many years ago in 1954—The Bride's Cookbook tucked away in my suitcase under my new maternity clothes.

I had been in touch with Frank and Jenny's only daughter, Rosemary, who lived nearby with her family in West Long Branch, and was making arrangements for her mother, Jenny, to move out of the garage into a place of her own before the sale of the house. Later in the year, she responded to my Christmas card:

> When I read your card memories came to mind. Christmas morning my father taking my brother and I to your house. We would stare at that huge Christmas tree and think that we had never seen anything so big. Your mother and father always had a gift for us. Monogrammed robes stand out in my mind. They are fond memories. I never forgot those days!
>
> P.S. My son has been accepted into law school!

I remembered Frank, an Italian immigrant who spoke broken English and could barely read, and thought how proud he would be of his grandson if he were still here. My second thought: What an amazing country America is!

The property went on the market—"the last of the great estates" the newspaper ads proclaimed—but the town had become seedy and run down, and no longer attracted the wealthy families from New York with their lavish lifestyles. We finally sold it in 1992, two years after my mother's death, for much less than it was worth. Strangely, while driving back to my home in northern New Jersey after the closing at the real estate office a few miles from the property, I was overcome by a sense of relief. For two years Tommy and I had been responsible from afar for The Place—hiring a caretaker, arranging for maintenance and repairs, following up on visits from local real estate brokers. Now that was over; our tangible ties to The Place were finally severed.

We had emptied the house of its contents, each of us—Tommy and his family and I and my family—taking our favorite things. No one wanted my grandfather's formal portrait from the dining room; we donated it to the Long Branch City Hall, where it graces the walls with other dignitaries from the past. It wasn't long before we heard that the new owner had applied for a variance, planning to tear down the old, dilapidated mansion to make room for the twelve or more tract houses he wanted to build as an investment on the property. I assumed that the town fathers would never allow the acreage to be developed. That's never going to happen, I thought to myself.

*

With The Place no longer a part of my life, I was finally able to come to terms with the truth. Looking back in sadness, I was forced to acknowledge that some vital emotional nourishment had been lacking from what I had always chosen to think of—for the most part—as a magical childhood. There were tantalizing flashes of intimacy, but no flow of human warmth, no continuum of closeness and comfort. Any familiarity was inevitably abrogated. We never embraced and were never embraced. I never heard the words "I love you, Joan" from anybody. The word love was never mentioned to me at all; passionate feelings were never displayed; my personal feelings were never considered. Outsiders were hired to care for my needs. Some underlying trust was absent, and I never felt truly appreciated. I was both exceptionally privileged and indescribably starved; I was given the best of everything and the worst of nothing. But although I was never cherished, we all cherished The Place, and our reverence for its history and our immersion in its abundance covered up—most of the time—any sense of divestment.

I don't believe my parents were consciously aware of what they were doing. The emotional landscape they established felt both comfortable and essential to them. They were creating and extending a family myth, prolonging a lifestyle that they valued above everything else; unfortunately it included the repression of any intimate feelings towards me. Some of this was probably generational—the perpetuation of a Victorian upper-class belief, now outmoded, that a separation between children and adults was correct, that children should be seen and not heard. And all those trays— symbols of service, sociability, hospitality—had come between us, helping to build and sustain this emotional distance.

Rebellion never occurred to me. Caught in the time warp between the euphoria of the post-war 1950s and the violent, youthful revolutions of the 1960s, I was a typical member of what the sociologists had dubbed "The Silent Generation." My parents were never aware of my emotional isolation, nor was I fully aware of the deprivation. The sheer seductiveness of The Place overwhelmed— for the most part—the absence of love and affection.

Clearly, both my mother and father made me feel helpless, frightened and unprepared for the real world; neither one of them empowered me. But I can forgive them their limitations and insufficiencies. I know they didn't do it on purpose; they took over with the best of intentions. Besides, there is much to be thankful for. They were true patriots and instilled in me a love for my country and a profound respect for our Constitution and Bill of Rights. Education was important to them; I was given the finest undergraduate liberal arts education available to women in the 1950s. My passion for all the arts—theater and dance, painting, sculpture and architecture, music and literature—was nurtured during my eight years away at school and college—and continues to be nurtured. Fortunately, I inherited my father's intelligence but not his existential angst. And despite my mother's self-centered, hedonistic ways, beneath her selfishness I sensed a steadfast and generous spirit. I believe I possess the best of each of them.

I haven't gotten very far with my father's entreaties to examine other faiths away from the ancient faith of his forefathers. Although I have never denied my Jewish heritage, I still feel no allegiance to it. My passion for Catholicism was short-lived; I promised myself to see Bo and Jonathan through their respective confirmations at age thirteen, after which I turned into a "Christmas Catholic," attending Mass only on major religious holidays—Palm Sunday, Easter, and Christmas. Ironically, around that time the two priests at our local parish who had taught me instructions both left the Church to marry. Over the years since then, I've dropped out completely, disenchanted, like so many others, with the Vatican's ongoing, rigid resistance to liberalize the church's teachings on various social issues—birth control, abortion, homosexuality, priestly marriage, divorce, the ordination of women priests. Pope John's *aggiornamento* was not perpetuated by his successors. I'm not even sure organized religion—which so often throughout history has created wars, hatred, prejudice and persecution—will ever answer my needs. Today, as a lapsed Catholic, my spiritual search is on hold.

My outburst at my mother's grave seems to have unleashed an uncontrollable and unpredictable watershed of tears. Since that bleak spring morning in the cemetery in 1990, I have a tendency to cry easily, often at inopportune times. When something strikes me as sad or joyous or even funny, I start to gush. My tears may be triggered by something as simple as the refrain of a love song on my car radio, or by someone complimenting me on one of my children, or by the startling beauty of a phrase as I'm reading a poem or a short story to myself. Weddings are especially trying. While everyone around me is smiling, my tears flow as I'm reminded poignantly of the happiness—seemingly so available to others—that has eluded me thus far.

Occasionally my weepy moments are embarrassing, but they usually don't last very long. Now, with my sixtieth birthday recently behind me, I have adopted a philosophical view towards them. I think of my outbursts as not only my own tears, but also the tears that my mother and father, and who knows, even my grandparents, were never able to release during their lives—a torrent of unshed, atavistic tears stored up inside me, flowing out sometimes appropriately, sometimes inappropriately, as I enter this final triad of my life.

I worry, however, that I have unwittingly handed down to my six children this family pattern of emotional unavailability, this inability to cherish those closest, to make them feel valued—a pattern which I not only grew up surrounded by, but which I also perpetuated in my choice of husbands. We have started talking to each other about all of this. I hope that reading this story will not only help each of them to understand me, but will also enrich their own lives.

CHAPTER SIXTEEN

Declarations of Independence

—————

B y 1992, the year The Place was sold, our oldest son Bo had transferred from Vassar to Sarah Lawrence College—where, I soon learned, writing is a religion. When a brochure arrived in the mail from The Writing Institute (part of the Continuing Center of Education there) offering a journalism course—*Writing about People, Places and Things*—something clicked. I was still practicing residential design and had built up a roster of clients through referrals. With almost twenty years of experience behind me, I was suddenly inspired to write about what I knew best.

After studying for three semesters, I sent out proposals with sample articles enclosed, and was hired by a local newspaper to write a chatty column for their weekly home section—sharing helpful insider tips on decorating. Each week I wrote seven hundred and fifty words about a different aspect of design—Walls, Ceilings, Windows, Mirrors, Fireplaces—trying to get my reading audience to think about their surrounding spaces in uncommon and refreshing ways. Sometimes I wrote about a single color and how to use it—"The Power of Red," "Shades of White." Or I would focus on a specific space—"The Living Room," "The Dining Room," "The Powder Room," "The Guest Room." The question most often asked of me by clients during initial interviews over the years had always been: "Where should we begin?" One of my favorite columns was entitled "Start With Something You Love"—describing how a room could evolve around a special painting or rug or a featured piece of furniture—frequently a family heirloom. I loved the creativity and originality of the writing, and got a real thrill waking up on Thursday mornings knowing that the paper was on the newsstand

and that 35,000 readers in a nearby county would read—or at the very least glance—at my column, with my head-shot in the upper corner and an eye-catching color photograph of an interior accompanying the text.

In the meantime, as the years of our marriage spun out, Mike's dark side gradually took over my private life. Haunted by profound, unacknowledged feelings of worthlessness, his "moodiness" slowly spiralled into a vortex of intense depression and self-destruction. His erratic behavior intensified—he would gain a hundred pounds, he would lose a hundred pounds, he would gain it back again; alcohol and drug abuse would lead to periodic binges and disappearances from home. He would never discuss these absences, which must have included binge drinking, blackouts and possibly other women.

It was a secret, second life, but I was holding on to my denial; I kept trying to get him back on his feet, hoping to resurrect the man—and the marriage—of my dreams.

Over twenty-five years, Mike's career had slowly unraveled, his family relationships and personal friendships had crumbled. After a year's separation I had taken him back into the family in September of 1987, thinking that he had found some stability and truly cared about us. But I took him back too soon. He lost his job in December of that year when his department was closed down, and became increasingly depressed. Therapy, AA, rehab programs, and eventually—in 1991, a year after my mother's death—an extended stay in a psychiatric facility two hundred miles away, provided only temporary respites.

By Christmas of 1993 he had been out of work for six years and had given up actively looking for another job. Yet, despite my epiphany at the cemetery in 1990, I was still hanging on, still paralyzed, even though I knew that to save my sanity I would have to divorce him. At weekly sessions with Corinne, my therapist, I would acknowledge my procrastination, but would always find an excuse—a family wedding, an upcoming holiday—to postpone the inevitable, dreaded confrontation and ongoing negotiations with Mike.

"I guess you're waiting for a month of Sundays," she would comment patiently.

I had been working on and off with Corinne for over fifteen years. She had diagnosed Bo and Jonathan's learning differences when they were in elementary school, and had coached them, and myself, on ways of dealing with their weaknesses as they progressed through different grade levels. Bo had also shared with her his homosexual leanings as a teenager—and she had kept his confidence—long before he was ready to confront me and Mike with this reality. She had also helped me unravel the truths surrounding my "idyllic childhood" on The Place. Now I was depending on her to fortify me for my upcoming battle with Mike; I sensed that he would make it extremely difficult.

I was not worried that Bo and Jonathan, now in their early twenties, would be drastically affected by our divorce. Bo was wise beyond his years—along with "coming out" his freshman year of college, he had also been diagnosed as bipolar early in his sophomore year and had spent many months at home in recovery, trying to achieve his own stability through therapy and daily medications. Jonathan had also suffered from bouts of depression during his childhood and adolescence. They were fully aware of the ongoing family chaos caused by their father's problems, and had even accompanied me a year earlier to a consultation with a famous New Jersey divorce lawyer—to discuss Mike's deterioration and the denouement of the marriage. Bo and Jonathan had grown into intelligent, kind, sensitive young men; they didn't wish their father harm, but they agreed that to save myself I would have to dissolve the marriage.

Home for the Christmas holidays, Bo took a fresh look at what was going on—and had been going on for some time. Sizing up the situation, he gave me some new advice.

[176]

"Put yourself first, Mom," he said. "You never have."

It seemed like a novel idea. Then I remembered that thirty-three years ago—during my first marriage—I had also come to the realization that I had made a terrible mistake and had fought for my freedom. Bo's words inspired me to finally accept the truth—I was powerless over my husband; I could only change myself, not him. I was forced to admit that the man of my dreams had turned into a monster; I would never get him back. I needed to focus on rescuing myself, not my husband; I needed to reclaim my life. I decided to kick off the New Year by asking Mike for a divorce.

"I can't be responsible for you any longer," I told him on New Year's Day of 1994. "I need to be independent ... on my own."

"You'll never go through with it," was his immediate response. He must have been counting on his ability in the past to manipulate me, to tell me how much he loved me, to tap into my old feelings of inadequacy—allowing me to collapse once again into the passive mode of acceptance that had been instilled in me as a child. But I had come too far; I had endured too much with Mike. Bo had broken into my passivity and procrastination and had triggered my resolve. I was counting on my innate tenacity and resilience to see me through, as it had in the past when I fought to end my first marriage.

A few days later, Mike received a subpoena from my lawyer—who had been waiting for some time for my go-ahead—stating my intentions to divorce him and demanding his legal response. Realizing that I was resolute, he delivered his coup de grâce.

"I knew this marriage was a mistake two months into it," he told me. "I hate being in this family. I've never felt the same way about it as you have."

It was a shattering statement. True or not, his words hurt me to the core, invalidating more than two decades of devotion as wife and mother in one swift, harsh sentence.

Over the next thirteen months, enraged that I had the audacity to abandon him, and also terrified of being alone, he dug in his heels and refused to leave. We were polarized, living under the same roof but barely speaking to one another. The lawyers on both sides negotiated. Eventually, on a cold, grey February afternoon in 1995, I found myself sitting in a dreary room in the Newark courthouse—my attorney at my side, Mike with his attorney across the aisle. My lawyer had assured me that this meeting was a mere formality; we would only have to answer a few perfunctory questions and the divorce would automatically be granted by the presiding judge.

I should have felt elated that finally, after all those arduous months, my wish for freedom would be granted. But suddenly, sitting in that gloomy courtroom, my body was wracked with wrenching sobs—the same uncontrollable weeping that had overtaken me at my mother's graveside five years earlier. Once again, my onslaught of tears was for the utter finality of what could have been and would now never be, not for what was over but rather for what had never happened. My early, fervent hopes for a happy, fulfilling marriage to the man of my dreams were a fantasy that had never materialized.

I was so convulsed that I was barely able to respond to the judge's simple questions. When he pronounced the divorce official, I felt a gentle tap on my shoulder. Looking up through my tears, I saw a uniformed guard motioning me to follow him down a side aisle.

"I'll take you to the freight elevator," he said in a consoling voice, leading me down a dimly-lit corridor. "Take it to the basement and you'll find the parking lot right across the street."

I made my way to the car, wondering how many distraught women, officially divorced for less than a minute, had been led from that courtroom by the kindly guard.

The court had granted the divorce, but—through psychiatric and vocational evaluations—had found Mike dysfunctional and unemployable. I was ordered to support him financially, not only for the rest of his life, but also after my death. Should I predecease him, my estate would continue his monthly alimony payments; I would be paying him, so to speak, from my grave. Emotionally worn out from a year of bitter disputes, and desperate for him to remove his hostile presence from the household and grant me some tranquility, I agreed to the terms.

I was sixty-three, Mike was sixty-one, when he moved out. He never spoke to me—or my four older children from my first marriage—again. He also ordered the members of his family with whom I had been friendly to break off all contact with me. But he stayed in touch with Bo and Jonathan, and relished making slanderous, insulting remarks about me and our marriage to the two of them, and to anyone else willing to listen. I knew from them that he was in failing health and was living reclusively outside of Boston, but even though we were completely estranged, his toxic aura hovered around me—exacerbated by the monthly alimony reminder on my bank statements, and by Bo and Jonathan's accounts of his irrational demands and misanthropic attitudes. I had broken my addiction, but I was still haunted by him.

*

Five years later, on June 1, 2000, I drove to the North Jersey Shore to attend a luncheon in honor of Lize's one hundredth birthday. She was having difficulty walking and was nearly blind, but her spirit was undiminished. We were all seated in the dining room of the Hollywood Golf Club, where she had been a member and an avid golfer—along with my mother and father—for most of her life. Lize arrived in a flower-bedecked golf cart to take her place of honor at the head table. She received the keys to the city of Long Branch from the mayor with unbounded enthusiasm, accompanied by a standing ovation from all her guests.

I was only a few miles from The Place; eight years had passed since it was sold. I had come to terms with its positive and negative influences on me, yet I still thought about it almost every day. But when I left the luncheon I did not drive by the estate. My mind was preoccupied with July on Martha's Vineyard—which would start off with our annual family reunion combined with Teke's three-day weekend wedding celebration. I drove directly to the Parkway, looking forward to the hour's drive home to review in my mind all the unresolved details of packing and preparing for the next month's festivities. The Place was the last thing on my mind.

CHAPTER SEVENTEEN

The Other Place

———

H igh-flying, fair-weather clouds drift over Cape Cod. The seas are light. Sailboats and powerboats flirt with our four o'clock ferry as it steams towards Martha's Vineyard Island from Woods Hole. Jonathan and I have been driving all day from New Jersey; my station wagon, packed for the month, is now safely stowed on board. It's only a forty-five-minute trip across Vineyard Sound, but once again—as on all previous crossings—as soon as I get up on deck and settle myself in the open air, I can feel all the stress from my hectic life at home draining out of my body.

It's July 1, 2000, the millennium year. Jonathan is twenty-eight; I'll be sixty-eight in August. On and off, for almost forty summers, I've been returning to this sanctuary in the sea—just seven miles off the coast of Cape Cod, but worlds apart from my everyday life back "in America," as year-round Vineyarders refer to the mainland.

Now, basking in the sunlight on deck, I think back to 1962—the year following my first divorce—when I was having a desultory romance with a man I had met at my brother Tommy's Brown-Princeton party the previous November. Peter's maiden aunt—his mother's sister—was a year-round resident of the Vineyard. At that time, in the early sixties, most people had never heard of Martha's Vineyard, or if they had—like me before I met Peter—they thought it was part of Cape Cod.

"I've got to get you to the island," he kept telling me. "It's the perfect summer place for you and the four kids. I know you'll fall in love with it."

Over Easter that spring, when my four young children were spending the holiday weekend with their father and his parents in

Washington, D.C., Peter and I visited his Aunt Kate on the Vineyard. As he predicted, I was enchanted; the following summer I rented my first house there.

That very first rental in 1962 was an old sea captain's house, a simple home of weathered shingle near the lighthouse in Gay Head (now called Aquinnah)—the most westerly tip of the island, isolated and sea-swept. The living room faced the Atlantic, and from the picture window the ocean seemed to stretch all the way to Spain. Behind the house, through a thicket of wild blueberry bushes, an ancient Indian graveyard stood on a knoll, reputedly haunted. At night, the lighthouse, perched on top of the nearby cliffs, flashed its beacon through our bedroom windows—guarding us, it seemed, as well as the ships at sea.

I was thirty years old, still recovering from my divorce from Red, hoping for a healthy, healing July and August with Ricky, Jimmy, Lisa and Teke—little steps ages three to seven—away from my broken-hearted ex-husband, my angry parents, my former in-laws who weren't speaking to me. My romance with Peter was short-lived, but my love affair with the island turned out to be long-lasting. The Vineyard and its lore got under our skin during that first two-month stay, and have been a part of our lives, off and on, ever since.

There was something magical about the place. Severed from the mainland, surrounded by water—the origin of life—the Vineyard offered a simpler existence and a serenity that came from being closer to nature. Not only was its natural beauty breathtaking, but also its daily pace was slower—a tempo reminiscent of an earlier time. Here it was possible to slow down and savor not only each day, but also each hour. Even our meals were simpler and fresher than meals at home. I soon learned that—with organic farms and farmers' markets nearby, and fresh fish caught daily in local waters—we could literally live off the land and the sea. On the Vineyard, the moon and the stars were brighter and seemed nearer to the earth.

That first summer we also learned that the island was not without its dangers. One afternoon, halfway through our stay, we came back to the house to discover that Teke's little red sneakers had been left behind at Menemsha Beach, eight miles away. My summer helper, Roberta, a reliable high-school girl from New Jersey, insisted on driving back to Menemsha to retrieve the sneakers, and Teke wanted to go along for the ride. The Gay Head roads are narrow and curving; Roberta, swerving to avoid a driver coming towards her from the opposite direction, plowed into a telephone pole. Teke was thrown violently against the dashboard (years before seat belts and airbags); he spent three days in the Martha's Vineyard Hospital with a concussion and a broken leg. My station wagon was totaled, as was the telephone pole, which my insurance company had to replace along with my car. I picked Teke up at the hospital in a creaky, old rental Jeep that I drove around for a week until a new car was delivered from "America."

The accident did not dim our enthusiasm for the island, however; there have been many other rentals since. The following summer found us in a snug farmhouse on South Road in Chilmark not far from Beetlebung Corner; the four kids could race out the door in the mornings for games and fun at the Community Center nearby. We rented there for several years, for the most part a happy, carefree time.

But one afternoon in 1963, during our first summer in the farmhouse, the surf was kicking up after a storm had passed through in the night. Ricky and Jimmy were eager to ride the waves at Squibnocket Beach. They didn't last long in the water; it was too much for them. Lisa, not yet six, had barely mastered the dog paddle, but was begging to go in. Jane, my Smith classmate from freshman year on the fourth floor and a staunch member of The Rowdy Crew, was visiting. We were both strong swimmers, and decided to give it a try.

The waves were enormous and crashing; with Lisa in tow, we quickly realized we would have to get out beyond where they were breaking, where the water was deep but calm. At first, we were relieved to be beyond the turmoil of the heavy surf, where Lisa could paddle around on her own—even though the water was way over our heads. But our relief was temporary. Before we knew it, we were being pulled out to sea by an invisible riptide. The beach, the cliffs beyond it and the other bathers on shore (no on else was in the water) were receding from our vision, becoming smaller and smaller as we were pulled farther and farther from the shoreline. I could barely make out three orange dots—the brightly-colored hooded sweatshirts that I had bought Lisa's brothers earlier that summer so they would be easy to spot when I came to pick them up at the beach or on the jetty at Menemsha.

We started swimming back against the undertow. It was rough going for me; I was hampered with Lisa under one arm. Jane swam strongly a few yards in front of me. We were still far from the towering waves that separated us from safety on shore. I was beginning to panic, and I suddenly knew that I didn't have the strength to make it alone with Lisa. The water was still above our heads, and I sensed that I would need more than my stamina alone—if I had any left—to get her through that barrier of crashing surf to safety on the other side. If a wave tore her from my grasp, I feared that she would be dragged back out to sea and lost forever.

I cried out to Jane, still a few strokes ahead of me, "Don't leave! Stay back with me and help!" Jane turned around and swam back to join us.

Swimming side by side with Lisa still in my grasp, Jane and I approached the wall of waves, agreeing to take turns. The first wave pounded down on Lisa and me; she was torn from my arms. Jane and I, thrashing around in surf still over our heads, came up for air, desperately looking for Lisa. Finding her nearby, Jane grabbed her, and the scenario repeated itself with each oncoming wave as we got closer to shore. Finally, with Lisa in tow again, grappling with what I hoped was the last wave before safety on land, I lost her once more in the turbulent surf. When I surfaced I saw Jane on her knees in shallow water with Lisa clinging to her. I watched as they limped on to the sand. Knowing that Lisa was safe, I gave myself over to the now shallow incoming tide, letting the water push me over the bank of sand at shoreline like a piece of driftwood. My ankles were bleeding from the small stones and rocks that had banged against my feet in my struggles with the surf; mucus was dripping from my nose and mouth. I was shaking so hard from fear and exhaustion I couldn't stand up.

We had ended up about fifty yards further down the beach from where we had entered the ocean. The boys, who had been following our travails, were waiting for us there at water's edge—three little worried faces framed by their orange hoods. Slowly, I pulled myself together, and we made our way back down the beach to where we had started. The tide was coming in and the wind had picked up; Squibnocket had certainly lost its allure for that particular day. We packed up the cooler and beach towels and drove back to our cozy farmhouse—Jane and myself for a stiff Scotch. I knew that without her I probably would have lost my only daughter. The kids—including Lisa—were nonplussed about the incident. They were too young to understand that it had been a near-drowning. But Jane and I, despite our swimming prowess, never felt quite the same way about the ocean after that.

I never questioned my own survival—or Jane's—that day in the riptide. I knew I could rely on my physical stamina and inner determination to make it to shore. It was my daughter Lisa—not myself—whom I was intent on rescuing from death by drowning. During our ordeal, I was terrified of losing her, but it never occurred to me that my own life was in danger.

Over the years, that isolated, traumatic incident during the

[185]

otherwise tranquil summer of 1963 has taken on deeper meanings. On one level, it represents the most extreme boundaries of friendship. I don't think it ever occurred to Jane *not* to turn back and help. And over the past thirty-seven years she has remained a faithful and loyal friend, knitting Christmas stockings for all my children and grandchildren, remembering birthdays and graduations—and lately visiting the island for a long summer weekend with two or three other members of The Rowdy Crew, as we still refer to ourselves.

On a deeper level, in the process of rescuing Lisa I was unconsciously rescuing myself. Just a few years earlier, during my unexpected pregnancy, early marriage and divorce, I had already tapped into a physical and psychological fortitude that I was still taking for granted in the undertow at Squibnocket Beach that August day at the end of my thirtieth year. I didn't know it then, but during the years ahead I would need to turn to those qualities over and over again, fighting certain emotional currents that threatened to pull myself and my children under.

I rescued my only daughter, I rescued myself, and I also rescued the child in myself. The sense of wonderment that was instilled in me as a young girl on The Place would continue to be nourished on the island. During each summer visit I would be filled with a sense of awe at the duality of nature—both its raw, unpredictable power and its precarious, delicate beauty. And over the years—in different ways—the healing powers of the Vineyard would continue to rescue both me and my family from the emotional turmoil surrounding our everyday lives "in America."

*

As the ferry plows its way across the sound and the island comes into view, Jonathan and I continue to unwind from our drive. Plump seagulls hover near us above the railings, anticipating snacks from passengers on deck. I'm remembering how my second marriage in

1967 brought an end to my summer rentals. Mike did not share my enthusiasm for the Vineyard; he had no special warmth in his heart for the island. At his suggestion, however, in the summer of 1978, when our sons Bo and Jonathan were nine and six, we rented a house in Chilmark for ten days. Perhaps he was trying to please me; perhaps he just wanted to give it another try—he never explained. But a spate of overcast weather reinforced his dislike of the place. He regarded the Vineyard as a nuisance—difficult to get to from his office in New York City, a destination where the *New York Times* and the *Wall Street Journal* were overpriced and not readily available early each morning. A "meat and potatoes man," he wasn't thrilled with our daily regime of pastas, fresh fish and organic vegetables, either.

Eight years later, however, in 1986, when Bo graduated from the Trinity-Pawling School, he and seven other classmates rented a house on the island in Vineyard Haven for the summer. I flew up for a long weekend with Jonathan, then fourteen; we drove around in our rental car, revisiting each one of the seven distinctive communities that dot the twenty-mile-long island. As we found favorite haunts that we remembered from our earlier trip in 1978 and discovered new ones, we kept asking ourselves why we had waited so long to return to such a captivating place.

Meanwhile, at home throughout that summer, Mike's binge-drinking and disappearances intensified; I knew that I would have to find the strength to ask him to leave and try to stabilize his life—still hoping I could both resurrect the gifted, charismatic man I had fallen in love with and also save our marriage. Not able to rely on Mike and his judgments, I was making more and more decisions for the family independently. I decided to approach the children—the four older ones were now living all over the country—about a rental on the island the following summer.

Derrik (he had given up "Ricky," his childhood nickname), had settled in Vermont a few years after graduating from Bennington

College in 1977, where he majored in music, concentrating on composition and improvisation. He was pursuing his career as a musician, singer and songwriter. Jim, a 1979 graduate of Skidmore College, where he also majored in music, concentrating on classical voice, had left a job in advertising in New York City and was attending Stanford Business School in California. Lisa, a 1981 graduate of Hampshire College, had received her Master's Degree in Voice Performance the previous June from the New England Conservatory of Music in Boston. She was now living in Washington, D.C., where she hoped to start a band with a Hampshire College classmate. Teke, a 1981 graduate of Skidmore, where he majored in studio art, was pursuing a business career in Dallas. Bo was entering his freshman year at Vassar; Jonathan was in public school at home in New Jersey. All six kids were intrigued with the idea of a family reunion on the Vineyard if I rented for the month of August in 1987.

A few months later, on a warm, sunny Friday afternoon in late October, Lisa planned to fly from Washington and meet me on the island for the weekend to search for a house. I had not heard from Mike since he had left for work the morning of the previous day. I was nervous and worried and had barely slept the night before, but had made up my mind not to let his ongoing erratic behavior interrupt my plans. While I was waiting for a taxi to take me to Newark airport, he came straggling up the driveway, having walked the mile home from the railroad station. I suddenly knew what I had to do.

"This is it. We're finished. I want you to move out."

He reached out to hug me, telling me how much he loved me, promising that it would never happen again. There were tears in his blood-shot eyes.

"It's too late," I said stonily, and jumped into the cab that had just pulled up the driveway.

*

Lisa and I chose a contemporary house on Quansoo, several miles down a bumpy dirt road; it stood on a flat point of land dotted with scrub oak, adjacent to a gorgeous stretch of private beach. The following August of 1987, the two of us arrived together on the island; while we were unpacking a neighbor knocked on the door, inviting us to a clambake on the beach that evening. Sitting on the sand under a rising gibbous moon, the low tide lapping gently nearby, we dined on lobster, barbecued chicken, corn on the cob, and my favorite part—little mesh bags filled with onions, chunks of sweet and white potatoes, clams, mussels, and two kinds of Portuguese sausage. It was a magical re-entry to a place that Lisa and I hadn't shared on vacation since the summer of 1964, when she was almost seven years old.

"Mom!" she exclaimed suddenly as we munched away. "Let's do this for your birthday!"

Three weeks later, on August 19, surrounded by my entire family, including my mother and Mike (who had moved out that previous October, was working on his problems through AA and therapy, and was desperately trying to win me back), we celebrated my fifty-fifth birthday. We also started a tradition—the annual family reunion cum clambake.

*

As Jonathan and I cross Vineyard Sound today on the ferry, I realize, counting on my fingers, that this will be our fourteenth consecutive celebration on Martha's Vineyard Island. Since that summer of 1987, all my children—and assorted spouses, grandchildren, cousins and close family friends—have managed to come for a least one long weekend together. The island always surprises and delights us, and inevitably, no matter which rental house or what year, it seems I am always blessed with a month of healing and renewal.

Mike rejoined the family shortly after our month on Quansoo in

1987; I was hopeful that we could work things out. He knew how much my rediscovery of the Vineyard meant to me and all the children; he knew that I was planning to return the following summer, ideally not to Quansoo, but further up-island in Chilmark. On a bleak, snowy weekend in the winter of 1988, Bo and I flew up together to choose a different rental, this time for the month of July. He talked me into a two-hundred-year-old converted barn nestled in the Chilmark hills on Quitsa Lane. Filled with reconstituted attic furniture and musty odors, the bargain rental price was, for me, its only redeeming feature.

When we arrived on the first of July, however, Bo's prescient winter choice pleased me enormously. Breezes wafted through the open doors and windows of house, and even the furniture had a certain shabby-chic charm. Across the property goldfinches darted from tree to tree; a pair of red-tailed hawks was also in residence. At the foot of the lawn, an ancient, weather-beaten tombstone marked the burial of a sailor who had died at sea in the 1700s—most probably from smallpox. A hammock beckoned on the front porch, and the view across the ponds—dotted with sailboats—to the quaint fishing village of Menemsha, was picture-postcard perfect.

Outside the back door of the house, a dusty lane lined with honeysuckle vines and rambling roses led to a hidden but well-worn path. The narrow, overgrown track traversed a thicket of pines; it emerged at the edge of a jagged cliff, where a breathtaking view of the south shore suddenly came into view, as luminous as a Winslow Homer painting. Down a steep wooden staircase a secret beach stretched away, its sands spotted with dark glacial rocks humped like whales.

I spent six consecutive Julys in that house—until 1994, when I needed a larger rental for Jim's wedding weekend. He had stayed on in California after graduating from Stanford in 1987; his bride-to-be had fallen under the island's spell the previous summer. Mike had continued to deteriorate, and I had just started battling for my divorce when once again Lisa and I flew up to the island, this time to choose a house for the July celebration. It was another bleak, overcast January day, with the gray sky and the smoky sea melting into each other on the horizon. After many transcontinental phone calls, we settled on a large, contemporary house on a barren Chilmark hill. The home was lacking in charm, but its wraparound deck would be perfect for the reception at one end, followed by dinner and dancing at the other. We returned in July to unexpected island magic—from the deck, the ocean sparkled in the summer sunlight; the front lawn, where the ceremony was to take place, was encircled by a sea of gaily-colored wild flowers; an old chestnut stallion grazed peacefully in the rolling fields next door. I stayed there for three summers, then returned happily in July of 1997 to my funky barn on Quitsa Lane.

*

One July morning, a year later in 1998, I heard everyone in town— at the Chilmark Store, at Beetlebung Farm, at the post office—buzzing about the strange catch at Larsen's Fish Market in Menemsha. When I got back to the house on Quitsa Lane, I shared the news with my oldest son Derrik, his wife Marge and my three grandchildren, Jasper, Jovi and Sheyna —all visiting from Vermont. "Guess what? I hear there's a blue lobster over at Larsen's!"

A gifted musician, singer and songwriter, Derrik burst out laughing. "Only on the Vineyard," he responded. Then, chuckling to himself, he smiled and countered, "Once in a blue lobster." I wondered if a song was in the making.

After lunch, we decided to drive over to Menemsha to have a look. Sure enough, a one-and-a-quarter-pound chicken lobster the color of lapis lazuli was nestled in the bottom of the tank, glowing like a jewel among its sinister black contemporaries. Not only was the lobster a deep cobalt blue, but also the feathery edge of its tail was bright yellow. The rare crustacean had been caught by a local fisherman in his trap; a few days later it was shipped to the Woods Hole Aquarium, where as far as I know, it still resides. According to marine biologists, this unusual mutation occurs about once in thirty million lobsters. But for me, more than a quirky phenomenon of nature, this was one more piece of island magic to add to the growing list.

A few days later, at the very end of my July stay, Teke came over from his own rental house for a farewell supper on my porch on Quitsa Lane. Since graduating from college in 1981 until just a few years ago, his life had been tumultuous. While working on his career as a salesman in Manhattan, he struggled with substance abuse for a number of years, almost dying from an overdose. In 1984 he left for Dallas in a desperate attempt to move away from his drug contacts in New York City, and also to start a new career in the business side of television. His TV work took him to Los Angeles for several years, then to San Antonio; during that time he was able to overcome his substance abuse. (I did not know about Teke's drug addiction and near-death overdose until he was in recovery and shared his story with me when I visited him in Los Angeles). Drug-free, on a business trip to Houston from San Antonio in October 1990, he was almost killed when a pick-up truck running a red light plowed into him on the passenger side of a car taking him back to the airport. His injuries were severe: a fractured pelvis and a flail chest—a life-threatening condition that occurs when the chest cavity is crushed by broken ribs, resulting in a collapsed lung and internal bleeding. Once again his resilience prevailed; after several weeks in a Houston hospital in excruciating pain, he recuperated at home in San Antonio, where Lisa visited to aid and comfort him. Back on his feet, he moved to Dallas to start his own video production company with a new friend as a business partner.

Recently he and his partner had sold their successful company in Dallas. He was leaving the island the next day for Baltimore—

to visit Lisa and look at a vintage Cadillac to add to his car collection—before returning to Texas. (Lisa had moved to Baltimore from Washington in 1989; she was still pursuing her music and also working for Young Audiences, a national not-for-profit organization that brings various arts programs into the public schools).

Only the two of us were left from the family reunion, and as the sun sank over the Chilmark hills, we sipped our Chardonnay and shared one of our favorite island dinners—freshly-caught swordfish, home-baked bread and fresh pesto from the Farmers Market, organic island greens lightly tossed with my homemade vinaigrette dressing. I don't remember our exact conversation, but we talked into the night, as crickets chirped nearby in the bushes and fireflies danced in the air. I remember Teke asking me many questions about my parents and grandparents; about my childhood and also his; about my two marriages and divorces. I remember feeling very laid back, very close to the earth, very open. A few weeks later, back in New Jersey, I received a surprising letter from him written on his birthday:

September 8, 1998

Mom,

I have wanted to write this letter since our conversation my last night on the Vineyard. I am not sure how much of that conversation you remember but we were talking about childhood issues. I guess we talked about different childhood issues (both yours and mine) the entire month but this particular night you said some things that hit me particularly hard. Basically, you apologized for not being the mother you had hoped you would be. I am oversimplifying what you said but that was the general tone.

I have intellectually accepted the fact that all of my parental figures did the best they could but there has always been a big separation between what I intellectually accept and understand and what I embrace in my heart. There was something in your words that night, your willingness to take full responsibility for your actions, that has truly set me free.

From the Vineyard I went to Baltimore to visit Lisa and buy another Cadillac. . . . Lisa had some wonderful pictures of us as young children (between 5 and 12). I looked at those pictures of the two of us and another light went on. I was a happy child. The kid in those pictures was thriving. We both were. My problems did not start until my adolescence. I guess everyone's adolescence is tough and mine was exacerbated by Mike Bowman's alcoholic demeanor but that is a whole separate issue. The fact was you were doing a great job, as a single mother, with four kids, in a time when this was not very accepted or glamorous behavior. I guess what I am trying to say, is that I applaud you. You took on a very difficult job alone and did it well. Kids need two parents and although we didn't have that we did have one, who during our formative years helped us all become the caring and intelligent people we are today.

So here it is the evening of my 39th birthday. Tonight I am sitting alone in a lovely suite in the Plaza Hotel in NY. Not the best way to spend a birthday but then, far from the worst. If it had been up to me I never would have written my life this way. The road that has brought me here has been a twisty one and I do hope that there is a lot of road still to travel. But either way, today I am happy. I am happy partly due to your efforts. You have taken on a lot in your life. I guess your children are the last to ever recognize that.

What I want to say is thank you. Thank you for caring. And thank you for opening yourself up and revealing what I know are painful feelings. It meant a lot to me and always will.

Teke

Teke's letter overwhelmed me and brought tears to my eyes. Once again, the island had worked its magic—this time, on a moon-lit July evening, not a miracle of nature but an unexpected bonding between a mother and son.

*

As Jonathan and I head out from the ferry slip in our car, the temperature hits eighty degrees. From Vineyard Haven, the harbor town where the ferry has docked, it's a twenty-minute drive up-island the rolling hills of rural Chilmark. I turn off the air conditioning and lower the windows. Rambling roses are in full bloom on fences and doorways as we pass the outskirts of town. The scents of honeysuckle and new-mown hay drift in through the open windows of our station wagon. We pass the Allen Farm, just a few miles from the turnoff to our own rental. Horses wander freely through the fields, and plump sheep bleat at their lambs in the warm, muggy air.

This July our family reunion will be incorporated into a wedding weekend. Teke, now a forty-year-old bachelor, is getting married to Kristie, twenty-five, a beautiful Texan of Mexican heritage who first fell under the island's spell when she first visited a year ago. Teke has rented his own house behind the Allen farm for his honeymoon. I am not returning to Quitsa Lane; the wedding for ninety guests requires more space both inside and out than that house and property can provide. Instead, I've rented a big, airy four-bedroom home at sea level on Stonewall Beach, with astounding ocean views from almost every window; old stone walls frame the property where the wedding ceremony will take place.

From my second-floor corner bedroom I could be on the prow of a ship—two walls are sheathed in glass, and the Atlantic spreads itself away, as far as the eye can see, to the gentle curve of the horizon line. I can watch the sun rise over Cape Cod to the east, and set over the Chilmark hills to the west. Along the jagged shoreline, past Squibnocket Beach, I can make out the Gay Head Cliffs, silhouetted in the summer sunlight. Upon sleeping and waking, I'll hear the constant sighing of the surf, as the tides, pulled by the moon, ebb and flow.

I'm hoping for more Vineyard magic this millennium July. But, whatever happens throughout my thirty-one-day stay, I know the island will reassure me—as it does every summer—that despite everything, there is some kind of order in the universe.

Our first rental on Martha's Vineyard near the Gay Head lighthouse, August 1962.

Back on the Vineyard on Quansoo for my 55th birthday: (left to right) Bo, Jim, Derrik, Marge, Teke, Lisa, Jonathan. In front: Jasper (Derrik's son) and Jovi (Marge's son).

Bo and Jonathan on Quansoo, August 1987.

The house and guest house on Quitsa Lane. We started renting there in July 1988.

Views to the east and west from the cliffs at Quitsa.

My cousin Nancy's children Sarah and Oliver with me on Quitsa, July 1997.

Members of The Rowdy Crew on Quitsa (Barb Churches on left flew in from Melbourne, Australia). July 1991.

Family portrait at Jim and Carol Roy's wedding, July 16, 1994.

My grandchildren Jovi, Jasper and Sheyna with Carol's niece Ashley at the wedding.

Bo and me back at Quitsa over Labor Day, 1999.

Teke, Bo, Lisa and me back at Quitsa over Labor Day, 1999.

The setting on Stonewall Beach for Kristie and Teke's wedding ceremony, July 8, 2000.

The Rowdy Crew and our friend Ann Holmes at Kristie and Teke's rehearsal dinner/clambake July 7, 2000.

Jonathan and "Mud,"
July 7, 2000.

My cousin Nancy with Lisa and me, July 7, 2000.

Kristie and Teke after the ceremony overlooking Stonewall Beach, July 8, 2000.

The Chilmark Writing Workshop: our leader Nancy Aronie on right in back, July 20, 2000.

Lisa and Buck on Stonewall engaged to be married the following May, July 2003.

My cousins Sarah and Nancy with me on Stonewall, July 2003.

The Rowdy Crew on the deck at Stonewall, July 2006.

On the deck at Stonewall, July 2007.

CHAPTER EIGHTEEN

A Millennium Wedding

t dinner together on our first evening on the island, Kristie, Teke, Jonathan and I review the wedding plans. The celebration weekend will start in six days with a welcoming Friday evening clambake, ending with a farewell Sunday brunch. Family and friends are coming in from all over the country. Three members of The Rowdy Crew are staying with me, always ready to pitch in and help out when needed. Tommy, Connie and their two married children are arriving; Red, now in between his fourth and fifth marriage, is coming from New York City; his brother Kin is flying in from California. His two children from his second marriage, Erica and Greg, are also joining us.

Both Kristie's parents are attending, but since a bitter divorce thirteen years ago, her mother has refused to speak to her father. Her paternal grandparents are flying in from Texas; they still speak Spanish to each other at home in the dusty little town where they live thirty miles south of San Antonio. A handful of her cousins and aunts from the Dallas area are also coming. Kristie is stressed with only a few days to go—worried about everyone getting along, about her hairdresser being on time, about the weather.

I try to reassure her. "Don't worry about a thing," I say. "The island always weaves its magic."

I can tell from the bleak look in her gorgeous brown eyes that she doesn't believe me. And I don't tell her that I feel just as stressed as she does.   *

A week later—on Thursday morning—I wake up early to a crimson sunrise, then deep blue skies overhead. The air is dry and warm;

temperatures rise to the high seventies by noon. I'm relieved; fair weather is predicted through Sunday. Wedding guests start showing up for the weekend; a friend from New York City arrives with her car on an afternoon ferry. I give her explicit directions to our Chilmark house. She calls a half hour later on her cell phone. "I'm hung up on a rock on Stonewall Road," she announces with a nervous giggle. Jonathan and I rush up the road in our car to help. The "rock" turns out to be a large boulder; the wheels of her Nissan are suspended over it; the car is immobilized. I can't help asking myself, "Is this a harbinger of the weekend to come?"

By Friday afternoon the big white tent has been assembled on the front lawn, its three peaks silhouetted against the cloudless azure sky. At five-thirty, our ninety guests start arriving for the clambake. For an hour, we sip drinks and munch hors d'oeuvres, mixing and mingling while admiring the astonishing view along the coastline all the way to the Gay Head cliffs. Mud, one of The Rowdy Crew, is regaling Kristie's mother, sisters and cousins with stories from her Catholic girlhood; Kristie's father has Teke and his friends mesmerized with tales from his years on the Dallas police force.

Without warning, an enormous black cloud appears out of nowhere over the house; I am struck by its peculiar shape, which resembles a whale. A few large raindrops fall. "Just passing over," the bartender assures me. Moments later, a violent squall envelops us with high winds and torrential rain. We rush to the tent and quickly roll down the sides to ward off the gale. The platters are ready, buffet-style, overflowing with seafood and barbecued chicken and corn on the cob. I move from table to table, showing the Texans how to dissect a lobster, coaxing them to try a steamed mussel or clam from the little mesh bags. There's high festivity in the air. Suddenly, the storm stops, the skies clear, and arcing up to the heavens, forming a huge semi-circle over the horizon, is a full, double rainbow. Everyone rushes outside the tent in the middle of dinner to witness this breathtaking sight. That's when I know that the island's magic has taken over—and I don't have to worry about the weekend anymore.

Saturday is sunny and breezy all day. By six o'clock we are all seated in white folding chairs on a corner of the property facing the glistening sea. John Alley, a justice of the peace who has performed over a thousand weddings on the island, presides in top hat and tails, looking very Lincolnesque. At the end of the seven-minute ceremony, he recites an ancient Apache wedding prayer:

> Now you will feel no rain,
> For each of you will be shelter to each other.
> Now you will feel no cold,
> For each of you will be warm to each other.
> Now there is no loneliness for you:
> There is no more loneliness.
> Now you are two persons
> But there is one life before you.
> Now go to your dwelling place
> To enter into the days of your togetherness.
> May your days be good and long upon the earth.

By seven o'clock, the cocktail hour on the lawn is over; we are all assembled for dinner and dancing under the tent. The scent of roses and lilies drifts in the air; votive candles twinkle on the round tables as the sun sets. Derrik has brought his band from Vermont, and the music is taking off with a reggae beat. The bride's eyes sparkle as she and the groom take to the dance floor. Their joy is contagious. After all the planning—and worrying—this wedding has taken on a life of its own.

The following morning, a hot summer sun prevails. I sit with The Rowdy Crew on the patio of the house behind the Allen Farm that Teke and Kristie have rented for their honeymoon. Blue-and-white-checked tablecloths dot the tables; the reassuring smell of freshly brewed coffee wafts on the breeze as we wait for brunch guests to arrive. Nearby on the farm, sheep still bleat in the warm, muggy air and horses still wander through the fields. Guinea hens flutter in the hedges; a late-rising rooster crows his blessing. I close my eyes and bask in the sunshine, the highlights of the weekend blurring pleasantly in my mind: sunlight and squall, moonlight and roses, a double rainbow, an Apache prayer. I'm winding down; I'm coasting; I'm full of contentment.

For Tuesday's session, I have combined yesterday's first assignment in class, "Dinner at My House—Family of Origin," with our homework assignment, "I Wasn't Invited." I write about not being invited to join my parents for dinner in their elegant dining room during my childhood on The Place. I describe being relegated to eating in the card room with Tommy and Mamzelle—ending with the pea soup episode and the humiliation and isolation I felt. I'm starting to open up.

Diane, in her mid-thirties, a medical writer and young mother from Newton, Massachusetts, ignores the homework assignment and reads a harrowing description of the birth of her beloved daughter, Kyra, a year and a half ago. John, in his mid-sixties, the head of the English department at the Martha's Vineyard High School, looks startled when he hears the name Kyra. He explains haltingly that *his* beloved daughter, Kyra, an only child, was killed in an automobile accident ten years ago. He is still so haunted by the loss that, until today, he has talk not been able to either talk or write about it. He is hoping the workshop will jump-start his feelings and enable him to exorcise his anguish.

Lisa reads aloud: "I was seven. My parents had been divorced for several years—maybe four—and I loved my Dad ... His girlfriend, Cay, was glamorous. She looked perfect in the front seat of his Mercedes. I wanted her to like me. I wanted her to teach me to be like her." I have never heard this story before; my stomach churns, my face tightens. Everyone in the group is staring at me, registering my reaction. Lisa continues, "I don't remember how I found out they were going to be married ... I would fantasize about living with them ... she would brush my hair and we'd go out to dinner every night ... I dreamed about how beautiful their wedding would be ... maybe I would get to be the flower girl ... Then one Saturday my father and Cay came out from the city to New Jersey to see us ... big smiles ... stories about this and that town in Spain ... and I realized they were married." Lisa hesitates, takes a deep breath. "And my brothers and I had been totally left out—uninvited. The first time I realized we had no real place in my father's life."

The group is silent, speechless; I am stunned, shattered. Forty years have passed since I broke up a family against everyone's wishes. Now the horror of it all comes sweeping back over me—how my husband Red desperately tried to prevent it; how my parents were furious at me; how my in-laws stopped talking to me; how my four children were forever scarred. And how—even after all these years—I still wish it could have been different.

Toward the end of class, we are asked to write about "I'm Sorry." Mary, a school social worker in her early thirties from St. Paul, Minnesota reads: "I am sorry ... and I am not sorry. Paradox. I am sorry that in coming out as a lesbian I have lost my family of origin." Her voice cracks and she reaches in her pocket for a tissue. "Six siblings, six in-laws, fifteen nieces and nephews and two parents ... But I am *not* sorry for me. I am healthy now ... I have come home."

Since writing "Returning Things" yesterday, I've been thinking about the emotional drainage of my two divorces on myself, my two former husbands and each of my six children—all the turmoil. I'm also thinking how fortunate I am to still be tall, strong and healthy, and also to have all the kids—now twenty-eight to forty-seven—in close contact with me and each other. Lisa's reading this morning reminds me that although I initiated both divorces for my own sanity, and despite Teke's heartfelt letter two years ago, I still carry a residue of guilt that makes me feel unworthy of being loved by my children. I read aloud: "I'm sorry for the heartbreak I caused my six children ... my two husbands ... for what I did to eight souls, eight spirits. But I'm not sorry for myself ... I'm the lucky one ... " Suddenly I start sobbing uncontrollably and bury my face on Lisa's shoulder. She puts her arm around me until I calm down.

On the way home in the car, I apologize to Lisa for being out of control. "Mom, you're such a good writer. It's really good that you're getting all these feelings out." I bask in her praise, and I realize we've never shared anything like this before.

My outburst today in the workshop has made me realize I have to go beyond my craft and consistently access my inner emotional life. I have to stop "stuffing" my feelings; I have to get rid of the guardedness and repression that I've inadvertently carried with me since my isolated childhood and that I comfortably fall back on in my work. I know that reaching this level is essential to my best creative writing.

It's a breakthrough, and for the Tuesday evening homework assignment, "A Fight in a Car," I recreate an emotionally charged argument with Mike a few years into our marriage that left us completely polarized—with him completely self-absorbed and oblivious to my feelings, and myself deeply skeptical about the future of our marriage. I'm beginning to dig deeper.

By Wednesday morning—our third get together—John has put his daughter Kyra's death on paper for the first time. As he reads, his voice quavering, we are all engulfed in the immense grief that has "turned the lights of [his] universe off and wrapped [him] in darkness," rendering "each second [of each day] an eternity of suffering." When we break for bread he is already standing inside the kitchen door. We file in, one by one, hugging him and murmuring our sympathies. I feel as if I'm attending a wake.

Back in our chairs, Nancy thanks us for our generosity and our willingness to feel the pain. "Emotional risks and creative risks are one and the same... Thank you for honoring each other." Then a change of pace. "Spend the next five minutes writing about "Shoes," she orders.

We're all ready for a lighthearted subject after John's traumatic story. I write, "I'm told that shoes—high-heeled shoes, that is—are supposed to be sexy. Well, that let's me off the hook ... When I try to walk in spike heels I tilt back and forth like the QE2 in high seas."

Stockton writes, "Shoes, what a screwy topic. But shoes are like a foundation ... They ground you in the present ... I remember laughing when I first heard someone describe a woman's stiletto heels as 'come fuck me shoes'..."

Then Lisa reads: "My earliest memory is my father's shoes coming down the stairs of our house ... I'm on the floor or maybe in a playpen ... then we're in the breakfast nook—sun shining in—S U N - S H I N E!—and messy table, high chair, gooey warm cereal from Mom. Mom making, serving, being. Happiness."

Suddenly I am face-to-face with the sunny nature my daughter was born with—the joy that has always been in her soul and is still bubbling over. I recognize that despite all the ups and downs, she always loved me and still loves me. I'm overwhelmed; my tears well up again.

At dinner that evening, she tells me what a powerful experience the workshop is for her. "All the voices opening up. All the honesty. I have so many new ideas for my songwriting," she says.

We're all geared up for our last session on Thursday morning. The past three days have been increasingly intense—as we laugh and cry and continue to pour our feelings onto paper. I am writing in class; I am writing at home; I am heady with confidence.

I'm also feeling emotionally wiped out; I don't want to tap into any more sensitive areas. I bypass the assignment, "What I Should Have Said," and read aloud "Island Miracles"—my essay that appeared in the *Gazette* two years ago—hoping to inspire others in the group to send off their work for publication. When it's Lisa's turn she reads, "This is a precious moment ... I want to thank all of you for all that you've given... I want to leave something in the circle. I think I need to sing." She takes our breath away with a passionate rendition of "But Beautiful," an old standard by Johnny Burke and Jimmy Van Heusen. Even Nancy is teary-eyed at the sheer magic of this totally unexpected, serendipitous moment. I am so proud of my only daughter and her singing heart.

After we break bread, Nancy sends us back to our chairs for the last time. "You have six minutes. Write about 'I Want to Remember.'" This one is easy. I write quickly and fluidly, and when it's time to read aloud I ask to go last, sensing that my words will stand as a fitting coda to our four mornings together here under the pine tree. Stockton wants to remember "what really matters, what's really real, what's important ... so I don't have to walk this path again." Diane wants to remember her grandmother Kyra's recipes "because I need to remember her, and her namesake does too." Today is Mary's birthday; she is hoping to move to the island permanently if she can get a job with the public school system. She wants to remember "it is my life to CREATE and TRUST and LIVE." Coincidentally, John's Kyra would also be celebrating a birthday today—her nineteenth, if she were still alive. He reels off a lyrical list of "I want to remembers" including the taste of fresh pesto on his tongue and the first time he met Nancy Slonim Aronie. Lisa wants to remember "that I'm strong enough to walk into anything and smart enough to know when to walk away ... that I now know what it means to speak with your heart *and* your mind ... Put your toe in and swim." Then it's time for my farewell:

I want to remember these past four mornings ... the tears and the laughter, the secrets and the sharings, the humor and wisdom of our leader and guru, allowing us to write from our hearts.

I want to remember my beautiful daughter, Lisa, on this our last morning, singing from the depths of her soul, her tremulous voice piercing the breeze.

The traffic whizzing by on South Road reminds us of the outside world – frantic, noisy, scary. But inside our circle, under the pine tree, miracles have happened this week. Here our language becomes sacred, every word offered up like a prayer.

July 20, 2000. West Meadow. Chilmark. Martha's Vineyard

Island. I want to remember ... I am a writer. I want to remember ... I am truly blessed.

Nancy speaks to us for the last time: "Every one of your voices has been distinct and clear and individual and filled with power and courage. We mined for gold and we found gold. Give yourself permission to be who you are. Write your heart *in*, tell the truth and BE HERE NOW."

Edie and Stockton have invited all of us for a potluck picnic lunch; Lisa has to fly back to Pittsburgh at two o'clock for an early Friday morning meeting. We dash back to our house for lettuce, tomatoes, bread and Lisa's suitcase, then drive up the road to grab a bite with everyone. Soon it's time for tearful goodbyes. We have been so close for four days, but we know we will never all be together again.

On our way to the airport Lisa and I start talking about a celebratory vacation we've been trying to plan together ever since my sixty-fifth and her fortieth birthday three years ago—a trip we hope will bring us closer if we're alone together away from our boisterous, male-dominated family. Then it hits us, and we burst out laughing and exclaim in unison, "This was it! This was our trip!"

*

A week later, on the last Friday of July, I'm alone in the house on Stonewall Beach, looking forward to a quiet weekend. Jonathan— who returned to his job in New Jersey after Teke's wedding—will fly in on Saturday to help me pack up the car, and drive home with me to New Jersey on Monday.

It's been a full month. Friends and family, ninety-strong, have come and gone for the wedding weekend. Once again, the island came through with its magical surprises—providing us with the drama of a sudden squall followed by the blessing of a double rainbow during the Friday evening clambake. The writing workshop with Lisa was a special, intimate time for me. Now, sitting at the kitchen table around five in the afternoon, I'm catching up with the mail from home when the phone rings. It's Bo calling from New York City.

"Mom, are you sitting down?" he asks. "I have some ... bad news."

My initial thought: he must have lost his job. But I say nothing.

Bo takes a deep breath on the other end of the line. Then he blurts out, "Mike is dead!"

The shock is visceral. My heart stops beating; the blood drains from my head; I feel prickly all over. A sensation of lightness passes through my body and joins Bo's words—floating in the air above me. I'm having an out-of-body experience, but I force myself back into the conversation.

"Are you all right, Bo? Are you feeling okay with this?"

He answers me immediately, without stopping to ponder my questions.

"To tell you the truth, Mom, it's a relief."

Later that evening, I learn from Jonathan that when Mike's body was found in his apartment by his half-sister, the shower was running; the TV was on; he had been dead for at least a week. These morbid details are a chilling coda to my years of continuous giving and his relentless disintegration. But Bo is right. It's a relief; it's a blessing; it's a gift. Mike's death has set me free.

CHAPTER TWENTY

The Final Farewell

————

On a balmy morning the following May 2001—almost a year after Mike's death—I head south on the Garden State Parkway from my home in northern New Jersey to attend Lize's memorial service; she lived to be almost a hundred and one. My brother Tommy has driven down from Connecticut, and we gather with fifty or so family members and friends under a small tent in her garden on Pullman Avenue in Elberon to pay our last respects.

I can smell the salt in the soft spring air. Just a few blocks away, down the street from the garden, the Atlantic spreads itself to Spain. The Ocean Beach Club—where Tommy and I learned to swim in the saltwater pool, where my father struggled with his physical therapist to get his shattered leg working again—is right around the corner.

Looking around, I recognize younger friends and acquaintances of my mother's—now not so young—many of whom had attended her memorial service or had written letters of condolence to Tommy and me, eleven years earlier after her death in 1990. I know them all from growing up here on the North Jersey Shore.

Lize's great-niece, Mary—a childhood friend of mine—leads us through a series of humorous and touching reminiscences involving her great-aunt's long life, which spanned the twentieth century. Mary takes us from Lize's young adulthood when she lived with her parents on their estate nearby, through her happy marriage in middle age, her ongoing life with her husband Barry in the charming cottage adjacent to the garden, and her widowhood, culminating with her final honor—receiving the keys to the city of Long Branch from the mayor on her one-hundredth birthday a year earlier. When the nostalgic service ends, I decide to take a short detour and drive by The Place, instead of going directly back to the Parkway; the property is only a few miles from Lize's cottage.

I have not been back since the house was sold and emptied out nine years before. During those years, I battled for my divorce from Mike, established an independent lifestyle, strengthened my ties with my six children. I've been designing rooms; I've been working on my writing. And I believe I've come to terms with what was missing from my childhood on The Place.

Still, as I approach the estate in my car, I'm overtaken with nervousness. My heart starts pounding and my palms on the steering wheel become damp with sweat. I'm suddenly fearful of what I'm about to discover, and I wonder if I should turn around. But I've already reached the western edge of the property. My eyes catch sight of The Little House—set in from the corner on a small rise—the house my grandfather Clarence had built for Virginia, my mother's older sister, on the occasion of her first marriage in 1919.

It looks ramshackle and forlorn, its white clapboard blotchy and weather-beaten, its windows boarded up, but it's still clearly visible on its grassy knoll where we used to go sledding sixty years before. Several new, modest houses, each with its own driveway and attached garage, now occupy the level acreage in front of it, facing the street. Looking ahead, I realize that the entire property is fringed with a series of these tidy little homes, each one slightly different from the other. I continue to drive around the old estate slowly, holding my breath, not knowing what to expect.

The stone gateposts are still standing, overgrown with moss and weeds, but the winding, gravel driveway—the original entrance to the property—has been removed. The huge purple beech tree, which had stood just inside the gateposts near the driveway like a welcoming sentinel, has been cut down. Many other large leafy trees that I remember are gone. Then I glimpse the dilapidated mansion, partially hidden from view by the dozen or more small, neat homes that surround it. Shingles are torn away from the roof; shutters are missing. The old house shimmers like a mirage; it floats in the soft spring sunlight, a fragile ghost of its former self. I imagine that a strong northeast wind or a hurricane gale from offshore might collapse it into a pile of rubble—wishful thinking, perhaps, that the knowledge of its non-existence, the assurance of its being forever gone from this finite world, would somehow soothe my soul.

But I tell myself it no longer matters. In the nine years that have passed I have deconstructed the power of The Place; I've come to consciousness about both its abundances and deprivations. The house itself is now a vacant, dilapidated shell; the ten-acre property has been desecrated; the physical reality of the estate is not relevant to me any longer. Instead The Place is now stored in my mind—pristine and protected from harm—where I can wander at will through its rooms and gardens, nourished when needed by certain selective memories. Once upon a time, the estate contained me, nurtured me, made me feel safe. Once upon a time, The Place possessed me; now I possess The Place.

I circle the property twice in my car. Then heading for home, I know there will never again be a reason to return.

CHAPTER TWENTY-ONE
The Attack on America

F our months later in 2001, on a gorgeous September morning—the kind that makes you feel glad that you're alive—I'm driving to the gym for an hour's workout at nine o'clock. It promises to be a serene, early autumn day, with summer temperatures and that special slanted clarity of sunlight and shadow that comes only as the fall equinox approaches. I'm still living in Short Hills, the peaceful, leafy New Jersey suburb, twenty miles west of New York City, where I've resided since my first divorce in 1960 and where I've raised my six children. From the highest hills in this tranquil town, the skyline of lower Manhattan is clearly visible.

I don't love these bi-weekly sessions at the gym; I'd much rather be home reading and writing. But this is how I try to stay flexible, to keep my cholesterol level down, to prevent osteoporosis—and so far, at age sixty-nine, it's working.

In the car I turn on the radio. "A plane has nicked the World Trade Center—probably a Piper Cub in training flying off course," a newscaster announces nonchalantly. I think nothing of it, but by the time I arrive at the gym, a small knot of men and women has stopped exercising and is huddled around the TV set that is suspended from the ceiling. I join them, watching in horror as flames and smoke billow from the North Tower. All we know is that a commercial jetliner has crashed into the skyscraper. When I get on the treadmill for my requisite fifteen-minute jog—still hypnotized by the images on the screen—a second commercial jetliner slices through the South Tower. I turn to the woman jogging next to me. "It's terrorism," we say to each other in unison. I have never spoken the word "terrorism" out loud before. "Nothing will ever be the same," I add. She nods. We are stunned, speechless; we can think of nothing else to say. We continue to jog, continue to stare up at the TV; we're like hamsters on a wheel, running numbly in place. I think to myself, over and over: this *can't* really be happening; this *is* really happening. It's a living nightmare.

When I move over to the stationary bicycle for ten minutes of vigorous pedaling, my eyes are still riveted on the screen. We hear that the Pentagon has been slammed by a third jetliner; there are rumors of a crash near Pittsburgh. I start thirty minutes of weight training, but I'm just going through the motions, frozen in this bubble of time on 9/11/01, paralyzed by the horror I'm witnessing. My safe, cozy house is only five minutes from the gym, but I can't tear myself away. With one minute of my session left, I watch the South Tower collapse like a house of cards.

Filled with terror, I rush home at ten o'clock to my own TV set, just in time to see the North Tower crumble into dust. Jonathan, now twenty-nine, calls in from his workplace in Edison—a twelve-story glass office building—half an hour away. He is living with me, working for a major real estate developer, waiting to leave for graduate school in a year.

"I'm on my way home—they're closing the building. We're on the flight path to Newark. Nobody knows what's going on, but we're all nervous as hell." I can hear the fear in his voice.

He takes longer than usual to get home. "I took a detour near the airport where there's a view of the skyline," he tells me when he comes in the front door. "I had to see for myself that the towers were gone." He shakes his head in disbelief.

We watch the carnage on the screen together; I cannot stop crying. How could the FBI and CIA not have seen this coming? What monstrous, diabolical minds have masterminded this grotesque crime against humanity? It's unspeakable and overwhelming; I'm sickened by it.

"I can't fathom the evilness of all of this," Jonathan says.

"Let's take a break for lunch," I answer as noon approaches.

We drive to our swimming and tennis club only a mile from the house. Sitting on the terrace, overlooking the pool where Jonathan learned to swim twenty-five years ago, we order drinks and salads and try to share our feelings. We are alone at the club; no other members have chosen to escape to this calm oasis. The manager comes out to greet us with tears in her eyes. "What a terrible day for our country!" she exclaims.

I think back to the shock and ensuing devastation of the Japanese sneak attack on the United States Navy that I remember so vividly from my childhood when I was nine years old.

"This is different from Pearl Harbor," I tell Jonathan. "That was a naval installation on the other side of the globe. This time we've been attacked on our own soil—twenty miles from our house! With thousands of innocent victims!"

I'm worried about Frank," Jonathan says. He's referring to a fellow-member of the community First Aid Squad who lives in town with his wife and two daughters and works for Cantor Fitzgerald in one of the Twin Towers. "He was so excited about working on the hundred and fourth floor—he couldn't wait to get there every day."

I keep thinking about Frank and all the countless, unsuspecting others who blithely went to work in the World Trade Center a few hours ago on such a gorgeous September morning. Suddenly it seems wrong for the two of us to be enjoying this bucolic setting with a holocaust raging nearby. We finish lunch quickly; on the way back to the house, Jonathan continues to reflect out loud—articulating what I imagine so many others are feeling.

"This is a turning point for me—and my generation ... All we've known so far is peace and prosperity ... We've been robbed of our innocence ... I'm wondering how we're going to live, day-to-day."

Back at home, all afternoon, we watch as the stunning images repeat themselves in vivid color on our TV screen. The World Trade Center is a pile of smoking junk; thousands of bodies are pulverized in the rubble. I know I'm still tall, strong and healthy, but I feel helpless, insignificant, useless and old. Nothing I've said, thought or written before seems to have any value.

On the evening news, I watch an innocent nine-year-old Manhattan schoolboy as he looks into the camera. "Why would they come and do a thing like this?" he asks.

Voices pour in from all over the world, sympathizing with America. But there is something else. We also hear that, across the globe, certain people are overflowing with secret joy over the attacks; in Baghdad there is actually dancing in the streets. It has never occurred to me before that we might be resented and despised by other nations.

Then I think back to another halcyon day—that clear, shining morning on the Smith College campus in June 1954—and to Alistair Cooke's commencement address. I rummage around and find the slim publication of his speech that has been collecting dust on my bookshelf for almost fifty years. Now Cooke's chilling, prophetic words truly resonate:

> We cannot wish that other nations become like us ... We must prove that the liberty of other peoples, and dependent peoples, is as precious as our own; we have to learn that real friendship springs from the awareness of differences and the respect for them ... You will have to be more sensitive, less patronizing to the feelings of other peoples, than any previous generation of Americans. If you are not, you will be hated.

Armed with and protected by economic and military might, I realize our leaders have not always been empathetic to other people's feelings, have not always respected their differences. Our complacency has blinded us to a new enemy of freedom—Muslim extremism. America has finally received its comeuppance. Our illusions of invincibility are permanently shattered. Now we're being forced to face our own weaknesses and vulnerability.

On a personal level, my life has changed irrevocably. I no longer feel protected by what I've always thought of as the greatest, most secure country in the world. Instead, uncertainty and dread prevail.

I've been accepted into the MFA program at Sarah Lawrence College; my first writing workshop meets there at ten o'clock the following morning, September 12. Manhattan has been sealed off; the bridges and tunnels are all closed. The only way I can drive to the Bronxville, New York campus from New Jersey is by taking a longer route, much further north, over the Tappan Zee Bridge. But I'm afraid to leave my home. For the first time in my life, I turn on the TV when I get up at seven in the morning and keep it on until bedtime—glued to updates on the catastrophe, waiting for and worrying about ongoing attacks. I know my "safe, cozy house" is now an illusion, but nevertheless, if anything else happens, this is where I want to be.

*

Almost six months have passed since September 11, 2001; rescue workers in the pit have finally reached what used to be the lobby of the South Tower, the first building to collapse. Just a few days ago, the remains of twelve more victims were pulled from the rubble— six civilians, five firefighters and one Port Authority policeman. Five residents of Short Hills have died in the Towers, including Jonathan's crewmember Frank; neighboring towns have lost even more.

But life goes on. Driving into Manhattan for dinner or the theater, I can see the pair of phantom lights reaching for the sky just behind Ground Zero. Installed as temporary memorials, they seem weak and ephemeral compared to the mighty steel and glass structures that once loomed in the space.

I know that I'm eating and drinking a little too much these days— it eases the sadness and anxiety. Bo and Jonathan talk about a subtle depression that has crept into their consciousness, an edgy nervousness that haunts them as they go about their day-to-day routines in Manhattan and New Jersey. Lately, they're not sure what they want to do for the rest of their lives; they're not even sure how much of their lives is left.

I wonder what my father would have said if he were still alive. As he aged, walking became more and more painful; he gave up the commute by train for a car and driver, continuing to visit his office at 45 Wall Street several times a week. By the 1970s, Cowen and Company had expanded significantly, opening in six cities across the country, and moving its New York City headquarters to One Battery Park Plaza, just south of the World Trade Center. By then he was in his eighties, fully retired and no longer commuting to the city. I thought back to his words during one of my visits to The Place shortly before he died in 1981. "I've gone from the horse and buggy to the jet engine," he told me that day, his voice tinged with amazement.

I'm grateful he wasn't alive to witness 9/11—that he didn't have to watch those two jetliners plow into Manhattan's tallest towers just a few blocks from Cowen and Company's headquarters; that he didn't witness the desecration of the Financial District where had worked for over half a century, that he was spared the loss of business colleagues and personal friends, that he didn't have to flee in a panic, covered with ash, limping in agony to safety uptown in a friend's apartment, or to a ferry or Coast Guard cutter along the Hudson River a few blocks away, to embark on the arduous journey back to the comforts of The Place.

My father had enough war stories for one lifetime.

CHAPTER TWENTY-TWO

Three Score and Ten

—————

By June 2002, we are still reeling from the horrific events of 9/11 that occurred the previous September. My seventieth birthday is approaching in August, and after talking it over with my family—my six children now range in age from thirty to forty-seven—I decide to go ahead with the party that I had been planning before the tragedies. We all hope that a celebration will lighten our spirits.

On Sunday, August eighteenth—the eve of my birthday—a crowd of ninety gathers around me on a chartered Hudson River yacht for a sunset cruise, with drinks on deck and dinner down below. As we sail around Manhattan Island—where my grandfather grew up and made his fortune in the nineteenth century, where my parents were raised and married in the twentieth century, where my father founded his Wall Street firm after the First World War—I am struck by how tied my family's history is to this great city. We cruise up to the George Washington Bridge, then down to Battery Park, around the tip of the island and up the East River as the lights of the skyscrapers slowly wink on. The Twin Towers are missing, but the cityscape is still breathtaking. During dinner there are unexpected toasts from my children and old college friends, and I respond to their compliments by reading an excerpt from Mary Oliver's poem "In Blackwater Woods":

> Every year
> everything
> I have ever learned
> in my lifetime
> leads back to this ...

To live in this world
you must be able
to do three things:
to love what is mortal;
to hold it
against your bones knowing
your own life depends on it;
and, when the time comes to let it go,
to let it go.

Toward the end of the evening, we slowly circle the Statue of Liberty, illuminated against the starry night—a gigantic, gorgeous, awesome sight. "The big, green lady in the sky"—that was my youngest son Jonathan's nickname for her when he was a little boy. Up on deck, Derrik, my oldest son, plays "God Bless America" on his guitar, and everyone sings. Then he plays Woody Guthrie's answer to Irving Berlin's "God Bless America," "This Land is My Land," and we sing again. "Let's sing 'God Bless America' one more time," I beg, not wanting these moments to end. Our voices join together one last time before we head back to the pier with tears in our eyes—tears of tenderness for each other and for our country.

Something comes together for me during this unexpectedly magical evening. Surrounded by a sea of people—children, grandchildren, clients, friends of all ages, even Mike's relatives, whom I had reached out to after his death—enveloped in a circle of love and affection, I realize that at least for tonight, the lost, lonely little girl who grew up on The Place, who didn't belong to the outside world, is gone.

*

Now, in 2007, my seventy-fifth year, I still think about The Place of my childhood—with all its sounds and smells and tastes that nourished me—just about every day. It is permanently lodged in a corner of my consciousness, like the nagging memory of a long-lost lover or a dead child. And my home is filled with mementos from the house—pieces from the past. A sterling silver Tiffany loving cup sits on a shelf in my front hall. Its engraving in block letters reads: "PRESENTED TO MR. CLARENCE HOUSMAN BY THE EMPLOYEES OF A. A. HOUSMAN AND CO. AS A TOKEN OF AFFECTION AND ESTEEM, JULY 22, 1911." My mother's bookcase is in my bedroom, my father's dresser in the guest room. I watch the evening news from my grandparents' old living room sofa, the sofa from my earliest childhood memory of skating with my father, the sofa where my mother always sat—recently reupholstered in deep red chenille. The blue and white willowware tea set from that memory now graces my grandparents' console table in my dining room. Around the inside of each gold-rimmed teacup, the dancing blue letters beckon me to "tak a cup o' kindness yet for days o' auld lang syne"—to take a cup of kindness for old times sake, for the years gone by.

In so many ways, my "cup o' kindness" is overflowing. I'm still tall, strong and healthy for my age; I'm still designing; I'm still writing. I'm visiting foreign lands with colleagues and professors from Smith College; I'm traveling across the country to family weddings and holiday reunions with my children and grandchildren. Derrik, my oldest Hoitsma son, an award-winning musician and songwriter, still lives with his family in Vermont where he teaches, composes and performs; Jim, recently divorced, is planning to marry his childhood sweetheart Pam—whom he found living half an hour away from his home in Los Angeles—and help her raise her three children; Lisa is now happily married to Dr. Attilio "Buck" Favorini, Chair of the Theater Arts Department at the University of Pittsburgh; Teke still lives in Dallas with Kristie and their two young children, Cruz and Pilar, where he runs another video production company. My first husband, Derrik Sr. (a.k.a. Red) is retired from Wall Street, now living in Sonoma with his fifth wife.

Jonathan, my youngest Bowman son, is on his second master's degree. He describes himself as "a humanist who believes in the capitalist system." His older brother Bo makes his living as a make-up artist, but he is gifted in many other directions—as a poet, an artist, a dancer, a comedian. Friends and family consider him a creative genius. He lives on the Upper West Side and is planning to marry his domestic partner Andy—an advertising executive—who has become a sixth son to me.

Sadly, my brother Tommy died of complications from Parkinson's disease in 2006; although I was never able to establish a close, on-going relationship with him, I like to think that he held a special place in his heart for his only sister. Happily, his widow Connie reached out to me shortly after his death, asking me to help with the renovations of her new house. We are now good friends, and attend theater, music and dance performances together.

And so it goes ... My life is full. Yet friends keep asking me, "Aren't you ready for a relationship after all this time?" "No," I answer. "I've fought too hard for my independence. I like being on my own—having myself to myself."

But I don't share the whole truth with them. I don't tell them that something is still missing. I don't confide that despite all the accomplishments and self-awareness, I am still grappling with an inner loneliness, still haunted, especially in my dreams, by fleeting glimpses of intimacy, elusive echoes of the joy I remember from that icy, glittery morning almost seventy-five years ago when I skated with my father—and more recently by the chilling thought that what I missed—in my childhood, in my marriages—will elude me forever, or that I may not be able either to recognize it or accept it should it come my way.

For after all, we bring to everything what we had before.

The Party of my Life

I t's July, 2008; I'm back on the Vineyard. I've returned for the ninth year to the big, airy four-bedroom house on Stonewall Beach where Teke and Kristie were married in July of 2000. My four children from my first marriage, now ages fifty-three to for-ty-nine, are with me for the Fourth of July weekend—Derrik with his wife Marge and my beautiful granddaughter Sheyna, eighteen, from Vermont (she is a dancer who will be attending Bennington College as her father did); Jim and his fiancée Pam from Los Angeles; Lisa and her husband Buck from Pittsburgh; Teke and my sweet-natured, tousle-haired grandson, Cruz, almost five, from Dallas. Kristie has stayed home with Pilar, just a year old; she's a squirmy toddler, not yet ready for long-distance travel. My two sons from my second marriage, Bo, thirty-nine, and Jonathan, thirty-six, will be coming later in the month. (Bo is still living in Manhattan with Andy; Jonathan is living in Denver after receiving his Master's Degree in Public Policy from the University of Colorado; his first Master's was in Real Estate Development from Columbia).

At dinner Sunday evening, everyone seems mellow—opening up, sharing and bonding. It seems to be a special time for reminiscenc-es and revelations. I drift off to sleep later that night, thinking that so far this is the best summer we've ever had.

*

The first worrisome phone call comes in the following morning. Bo has been ill all weekend with excruciating pain in his left calf, flu-like symptoms and an intestinal upset. His domestic partner Andy is on the phone from the emergency room at St. Lukes-Roosevelt

Hospital in New York City, where Bo has been taken by ambulance from their apartment on West 69th Street nearby.

Bo is a talented makeup artist; he is also a runner and goes to the gym religiously. By noon he has been sent home on crutches. Diagnosis: intestinal flu and also a muscle pull in his leg.

Andy calls again the next morning. Bo is feeling worse and has been to see his internist, who has sent him to St. Vincent's emergency room. "They're looking for a blood clot," Andy tells me, his voice tense.

The phone calls from Andy continue every few hours throughout the day—each one more dire and terrifying than the next.

"They're still looking for blood clots."

They're taking him into surgery."

"The doctors are mystified."

They may do open heart surgery."

"They may have to amputate his leg if he pulls through."

By late afternoon—with fear and uncertainty in the air—we turn to food and drink, sipping wine at the kitchen island as Jim, an accomplished cook, prepares a gourmet dinner with Pam . (Just about everything Jim tackles reaches perfection). There are only seven of us—Lisa and Buck have returned to Pittsburgh earlier that day. This evening we have forsaken our usual regimen of pasta or fresh fish; instead Jim is grilling côtes de boeuf—double-cut, bone-in ribeye steaks—while Pam puts together her version of "smashed potatoes" from a famous Napa chef. Freshly-picked lettuces, already thrice-washed at the nearby organic farm, are ready to be tossed; a fruit pie is warming in the oven.

Andy calls again. This time there is terror in his voice. "Joan, the doctors have told me to notify the family."

I put down the phone, frozen in disbelief. I turn to everyone. "What does 'notify the family' really mean?" I ask desperately.

We are all in shock, but during our delicious dinner, while we eat and drink, we plan. Bo's younger brother Jonathan is already on his way to Manhattan from Denver; Lisa is flying in from Pittsburgh. Jim, Pam and Sheyna decide to leave in two hours on a private plane to be at the hospital with them and Andy during this critical night. Teke will fly back to Dallas with Cruz as planned the next morning, then return with Kristie to New York to be with the family. Derrik and Marge will drive me to the city early the next day. I go to bed, hoping for a miracle.

At one o'clock in the morning I'm wakened from a sound sleep. It's Andy again. Lisa is with him at the hospital. "Joan." His voice cracks. "Bo is dead. Your son is gone."

Marge and Derrik have heard the phone ring and rush in to my bedroom. We cling to each other, sobbing uncontrollably. I'm numb with shock, but briefly come to my senses. I tell Andy to insist on an autopsy. Then I collapse on my bed, with one final, sensible thought. "I don't want Teke and Cruz to hear this until they wake up. Let's all try and get some sleep."

Miraculously, I sleep soundly for four hours. In the morning, I'm in the kitchen sipping black coffee, steadying myself for the trip ahead. I hear Teke sobbing in the upstairs hallway. Derrik must have just shared the terrible news. Then I hear adorable Cruz: "Why did Uncle Bo have to die, Daddy?"

What did I do to deserve this?

What did Bo do to deserve this?

I hate you, God.

*

On the drive to New York, I think back over Bo's thirty-nine years. He was always high maintenance—a colicky baby who slept inter-mittently, a hyperactive pre-adolescent with certain learning differ-ences. A talented artist with his own unique vision, as a teenager he made extraordinary greeting cards that were sold in a local gift shop. In college—where he studied philosophy, poetry and dance, acted and performed stand-up comedy—there were other challenges: coming out as a gay man, a diagnosis of bi-polar illness. I'm remembering all the ups and downs—but when Bo was on course he was one of the funniest, kindest, most creative people in the world. Everybody loved Bo. Why had this happened?

We learn later that he died of necrotizing fasciitis, commonly known as the "flesh-eating disease"—a virulent form of strep that usually enters the body through a cut or blister. Initially it attacks a muscle, liquefying it and often necessitating an amputation. If it's not caught in time, it rapidly attacks all vital organs. By the time the doctors recognized it, it was too late. Bo's kidneys failed; then his loving heart stopped beating, forever.

*

In the city, the family gathers along with Andy's mother and sister from Maine. Together, at the apartment on West 69th Street, we make arrangements for Bo's cremation and write the death notice for the Sunday edition of *The New York Times*. "Bo will always be remembered for his dazzling smile, wacky sense of humor, unique interpretive dancing and rampant creativity ... His greatest gift was making everyone he came into contact with feel special ... We have lost our spark."

Before we leave for dinner at a neighborhood restaurant (fifteen strong), Lisa looks over at me. "Mom, how would you like to give the party of your life?" She knows how much I love to entertain, but I can't imagine—at this devastating time—what she is talking about. "Bo would have wanted a celebration—not a funeral. You're the only one of us who can do this."

*

Back on the island for the rest of my July stay, I call the *Vineyard Gazette* to place an obituary. "Bo loved the Vineyard," I tell Julie

Wells, the editor. I explain how he came to the Island in 1986 with seven of his classmates who had just graduated from Trinity Pawling School. They rented a house on Church Street; he soon discovered the Vineyard Playhouse just a few doors away, joining Afterwords, an improv comedy group, and also performing Shakespeare roles over ensuing summers.

Julie has published a number of my essays in the newspaper in recent years. "Promise me you'll write about Bo for the *Gazette*," she entreats me at the end of our phone call. I think to myself: there *are* no words.

Jonathan and Andy arrive for the last week of my rental; we stare listlessly at the sea and start planning the celebration, set for August twenty-third. Condolences pour in from all over the world—by regular mail, by e-mail, by phone. The first handwritten note arrives from one of Bo's Trinity Pawling roommates:

> Bo brought so much love and joy to the world. One of my last memories of him was on the Vineyard. He insisted that Andy and I drive him to Lucy Vincent so that he could dance naked on the beach. Even though it was cold and it began to rain, this did not stop Bo ... Wouldn't the world be a better place if we could all just dance naked in the rain? I know Bo is doing the same in heaven.

I have never felt pain like this. I'm constantly weeping. I'm raw; I'm ravaged; I have no skin. Something has been gouged out of me. I contemplate suicide—to alleviate the pain forever—but realize I don't know how to go about it without inducing more pain. A huge, shaft of sunlight has gone out of my life—I'm living every day in the shadows.

*

We've chosen the Tavern on the Green on the edge of Central Park for the Celebration of Life to be held in Bo's memory six weeks after his death. It's a magical setting. A huge topiary of King Kong—benevolent, not menacing—stands guard over the flagstone terrace, where the spreading branches of a giant sycamore tree—rising to the sky—are laden with hundreds of colorful Chinese lanterns. On a nearby hedge, a large topiary of Peter Rabbit presides over the bar. Beyond us are the rolling fields of the park; surrounding us are the skyscrapers of the city.

We've incorporated Bo's unique art work into the e-vite and the program; we expect two hundred guests, but almost three hundred have arrived by seven o'clock on a warm August evening. After drinks on the terrace, we move into the Crystal Room—an adjoining glass pavilion where the eighteen-foot ceiling is studded with multi-colored crystal chandeliers—to sit for the service. I've asked Lisa's husband Buck—a professor, an author, a playwright, a Shakespeare scholar—to be the master of ceremonies. Buck is an eloquent man; I know I can trust him.

He starts off with a few introductory words:

> No life can be summed up in words, especially not the life of such a fabulous man, who lived so exuberantly, so companionably ... and who was so untimely ripped from the embrace of those who loved him ... Maybe that's why, when I learned of Bo's death, almost the first words that came into my mind were those beautiful words, spoken by Juliet of her Romeo, in that timeless drama of love and sorrow: "Give me my Romeo; and when he shall die, take him and cut him out into little stars. And he will make the face of heaven so fine that all the worlds will be in love with night. And pay no worship to the garish sun." When you look at the stars, think of Bo. Oh boy, did he twinkle!

Several of Bo's close friends, and my close friends, talk about Bo. Some of their reminiscences are excruciatingly funny, some are painfully poignant. Derrik sings "Standing Prayer," Bo's favorite of the hundreds of songs that he's written; Teke regales us with hilarious memories of Bo's childhood; Lisa and Jim sing "Close Your Eyes," a James Taylor song; Lisa reads one of Bo's poems:

HELLO DAY

At the start traversing a morning
Is hopscotch, a side-long rhumba.
My plans are big; lists fall
From the ceiling like heavenly
Accolades, kudos for the well-behaved.

Markedly ambitious and hawk-eyed,
Will I phone my sister for added support?
A run in the park shakes out my dreams
Hair becomes tendrils and packaged
Passion gleams bright.

In Japan three year olds sit in
sea-wide rows of violins. They have
no word for talent. Fluttering fingers
tiny like sparks strive and strive and
strive. God, I say, standing on the
corner, may all this love pour
into my hands, and please, please
make any difference.

Jonathan reads a short tribute to his brother:

I speak to you today as the only younger brother of Bo. Until July
ninth I never lived a day of my life without Bo—he was always
around. Whether nearby or far away, I always felt his presence
. . . I am not sure I can explain how greatly I appreciated his
amazing creative energy, his powerful charisma, his love and
understanding for all people around him. I can say that I was
Bo's number one fan—he was the funniest, most creative, most
talented man that I have ever known. And better still he was
my brother. I was truly blessed indeed . . .

We had a unique way of complementing each other; I could
always understand the technical aspects of life (like balancing
my checkbook, driving a car, having a good sense of direction
to get us from point A to point B). However, Bo had a sense of
direction when it came to human emotions . . .

Bo would want us all to enjoy life to its fullest and persevere
through the difficulties, as he so often had to do in his own life.
Let us do this in Bo's honor and memory.

I can't imagine how Jonathan has the poise to get up and speak, having lost his father in July 2000, and now his brother in July 2008. I am so proud of my youngest son, my four older children, my entire family.

Unlike Jonathan, I am too upset to speak; Buck has agreed to read a poem on my behalf. I've returned to Mary Oliver's "In Blackwater Woods," which I had read an excerpt from on my seventieth birthday cruise—Bo and a number of people here at the Celebration had heard it then. This time I quote the entire poem, which Buck reads with exquisite tenderness:

> Look, the trees
> are turning
> Their own bodies
> Into pillars
>
> of light,
> are giving off the rich
> fragrance of cinnamon
> and
> fulfillment,
> the long tapers
> of cattails
> are bursting and floating away over
> the blue shoulders
>
> of the ponds
> and every pond
> no matter what its
> name is, is
> nameless now.
> Every year
> everything
> I have ever learned
>
> in my lifetime
> leads back to this: the fires
> and the black river of loss
> whose other side

is salvation,
whose meaning
none of us will ever know.
To live in this world

you must be able
to do three things:
to love what is mortal;
to hold it

against your bones knowing
your own life depends on it;
and, when the time comes to let it go,
to let it go.

The program closes with a heartbreaking rendition of "Somewhere Over the Rainbow," sung by Victoria Cannizzo; Bo's partner Andy courageously accompanies her on the piano. Victoria—a stunning twenty-six year old friend of our family whom Bo has known since she was a young child—is studying to become an opera singer. Her vibrato fills the room to the rafters.

Almost three hundred people laugh and weep through the tributes, poetry and songs. We leave the pavilion for more drinks on the terrace while the Tavern staff converts it into a dining room for our buffet dinner.

Suddenly Bo's life unfolds before us on a huge television screen that has been set up on the terrace (another one is installed inside the pavilion). Teke has created a video of Bo's thirty-nine years; he has woven together photographs that we have sent him and has taken the background music directly from Bo's iPod. There is even a clip of Bo doing stand-up at the Gotham Comedy Club in the city, poking fun at his father and me. We all stand, drinks in hand, mesmerized by this astonishing work of art.

The husband of a Smith classmate who never knew Bo comes up to me. "Joan, I know your son, now," he tells me, with tears in his eyes.

Night falls around me, the skyscrapers wink on, the Chinese

lanterns glow, Peter Rabbit perches nearby, benevolent King Kong casts his lengthy shadow across the flagstone terrace. How Bo would have loved every minute of this!

*

A year has passed. It's July 2009; I'm back on the Vineyard. I still miss Bo terribly every day, but the psychic pain has diminished— it's duller, scarred over. I still weep, but I can also smile again; I can even laugh. And I can write about Bo. Yet the more time that passes since his death, the more senseless it seems.

I don't think about The Place as much anymore; Bo's death has taken over in my consciousness. Strangely, I never dream about him or even think about him in my sleep, but every morning, upon waking, a headline immediately wraps itself around my brain: BO IS DEAD. Nothing will ever be the same.

This July, I don't know if the Island can surprise me with the kinds of magical moments that used to lift my spirits—a cobalt blue lobster, a sea of gaily-colored wildflowers, a double rainbow. I don't know if I can be open to the magic.

This July, I don't know if the Island will reassure me—as it has every summer—that despite everything, there is some kind of order in the universe.

I do know that on the Island there's a serenity that comes with being close to nature. I know that its sheer beauty sometimes takes my breath away. I know that the tempo of life is simpler here. I can live off the land and the sea. I can savor one day at a time, even one hour at a time. I can try and live the way Bo would want me to live this first July that he's gone—here in this place that he loved beyond reason.

On the Vineyard, the moon and the stars always seem brighter, and nearer to the earth. I think back to Buck's words at the Celebration: "When you look at the stars, think about Bo. Boy, did he twinkle!"

On the first anniversary of the night that he died, I'll be on my deck near Stonewall Beach, looking up at the heavens—yearning for, reaching for, still trying in some mysterious, sacred way to touch ... Bo.